# GOD,
## ARE YOU REAL?

ARTHUR ADAM

BOOKS BY ARTHUR ADAM
Call Me Adam
God, Are You Real?

Copyright © 2016 ARTHUR ADAM
Written by Valeda Verrier
All rights reserved.

Published by ARTHUR ADAM
Layout and Design by Oak Island Publications
oakislandpublications@gmail.com
Published in Canada

ISBN-13: 978-1542401036
ISBN-10:1542401038

To my wife, to my church family, and to the ones that are hungry for God and will answer the call of God on their life.

# CONTENTS

|    | A Note from Adam |     |
|----|------------------|-----|
|    | Introduction | i |
|    | A Letter from Abigail | ii |
| 1  | Inspiration From Dominique | 1 |
| 2  | The End of the Stutter | 5 |
| 3  | The Power of Prayer | 7 |
| 4  | Tell My Mom! | 11 |
| 5  | Earning Grace | 13 |
| 6  | Leaving Home | 17 |
| 7  | Homeless | 19 |
| 8  | Meeting Lorraine | 21 |
| 9  | A Father's Love | 25 |
| 10 | God, Are You Real? | 26 |
| 11 | Call for Help | 29 |
| 12 | Help Offered | 32 |
| 13 | Speaking in Tongues | 36 |
| 14 | Don't Rely on Man | 40 |
| 15 | Questions for the Priest | 44 |

| | | |
|---|---|---|
| 16 | Professional Help | 47 |
| 17 | A Father's Bond | 50 |
| 18 | Altar Call | 54 |
| 19 | Fear Banished | 56 |
| 20 | My Brother Set Free | 58 |
| 21 | Belonging | 60 |
| 22 | Preaching | 63 |
| 23 | I Don't Want to Beg | 65 |
| 24 | Offended | 68 |
| 25 | The Prophecy | 71 |
| 26 | The First Clear Message | 74 |
| 27 | Purple Gas | 77 |
| 28 | The Spirit of God | 81 |
| 29 | God Heals! | 83 |
| 30 | A Voice Through the Crowd | 85 |
| 31 | God Speaks to His Children | 88 |
| 32 | The Tabernacle | 90 |
| 33 | Healing Laura's Leg | 95 |
| 34 | Seeing the Spirit Man | 97 |
| 35 | Called to be a Prophet | 99 |
| 36 | The Warning | 103 |
| 37 | Ultimatum | 105 |
| 38 | Rift | 108 |

| 39 | Walking Away | 110 |
| 40 | Betrayal | 112 |
| 41 | We Don't Have to be Perfect | 116 |
| 42 | Back Up What You Believe | 118 |
| 43 | The Coldest Night | 121 |
| 44 | The Pit | 125 |
| 45 | Balancing Accounts | 129 |
| 46 | Preparation | 132 |
| 47 | Two Cries from the Heart | 136 |
| 48 | Meeting Edie | 139 |
| 49 | God Touches Edie | 145 |
| 50 | Baptism | 150 |
| 51 | Ground to Dust | 157 |
| 52 | The Gift of Discernment | 161 |
| 53 | Ministering | 164 |
| 54 | Sharing Excitement | 166 |
| 55 | A Pastor is Chosen | 169 |
| 56 | Meeting Ed | 172 |
| 57 | Opening the Word | 174 |
| 58 | God Touches Ed | 177 |
| 59 | Shiloh | 181 |
| 60 | Driving Truck | 184 |
| 61 | The Messages Flow | 187 |

| | | |
|---|---|---|
| 62 | God Works in the Lives of His People | 189 |
| 63 | The Questions | 191 |
| 64 | Visiting the Colony | 193 |
| 65 | Baseball | 195 |
| 66 | Reaping the Rewards | 198 |
| 67 | The Mountain | 201 |
| 68 | Defying Gravity | 204 |
| 69 | Legacy | 207 |
| | Epilogue | 215 |
| | About the Author | 219 |

## A NOTE FROM ADAM

I want to help people. That's why I'm writing this book. It isn't about me at all. I want my stories to help point people to God. The first book, Call Me Adam, was about my fleshly life and the things I'd accomplished, but this second book is about the power of God, and His work in my life.

My desire for this book is to reach into people's lives and make them really question things: find out for themselves if God is real in their lives, question whether what they've always been taught is true, and seek out the answers. I know God is real.

He's proven himself over and over, and his promise is to reveal himself to those who seek him with all their hearts. God did not give something to me that he will not also give to you, if you pay the price and if you put him first.

I have no control over what happens with this book. God draws people and opens their understanding. I want the Spirit of God to lead this book to the people he chooses, just as he led Moses' basket through the river into the hands of the Pharaoh's daughter.

Please feel free to write me with any questions, comments, or concerns you may have. Please visit the Ekklesia Fellowship website to see some of the many messages God has given me to speak.

Email: edieadam@mymts.net
Website: ekklesia-church.org
Call Adam at 204-392-6767

# INTRODUCTION

There was a certain man called by God: a prophet and a messenger of good news to those who were in need. He walked through a market place one day going about his business. He passed by a certain stall where a crippled man sat, hunched over and deformed by a disease in his bones. The man, without thinking, reached down and with the power of Jesus lifted the crippled man to his feet. He kept walking as if unaware anything had happened. The crippled man's bones began to straighten, his joints popped into place—he screamed with amazement as a crowd gathered to see what had just taken place. The man of God walked on, then hearing the commotion, turned. He watched the once-diseased man leap for joy and shout about his healing. He looked down at his hands—had they just lifted that man to his feet? Everyone was looking for who had done this great deed, but he took no credit—none could be taken. If he had thought about praying for that man he would have doubted—how can someone so crippled be straightened and made well? He pressed through the crowd and walked on, praising his God who does miracles through us, despite us.

# LETTER FROM ABIGAIL

Hello Adam,
2010

I wanted to share something with you that really blessed me. You may think that your English is no good, and that you talk with an accent, but you have a way with words that I've never seen anyone have before! When you share about little secrets from the Lord, about experiences you have had, it is such a beautiful sound and it stirs up something within that wants to have that too, even if we don't fully understand it! Like on Sunday, you talked about the deep. I'd like to know more about it and how to get there, but to hear you say those things was more beautiful than any poetry written by people who have studied language. So don't ever be upset with your English, because you can speak better than anyone else!

I hope this encourages you!
God Bless!
Abigail

CHAPTER ONE

## INSPIRATION FROM DOMINIQUE

My shoes crunched and squeaked on the frozen snow and every so often I'd take a little run and slide on the smooth parts that were already worn down from car tires and boots. My sister Mona jogged along beside me, her short little legs trying to keep up. In the distance a crow called, and the air was so cold and crisp I was sure his call could be heard straight to Woodridge.

"I'm cold, Art!" Mona said to me, she had stopped to catch her breath and was clutching her worn jacket tightly across her chest. She had no hat, scarf, or mittens, and although there was no wind today, it was really cold. "Can we stop at Ma'Tantes today to warm up?" she asked pleadingly.

I knew if we stopped today we'd be late and I'd get a lickin' from the nuns. We were already running behind as it was. "Come here," I said, "You can share my jacket with me, but we have to run," I warned her. My coat was a hand-me-down and was big enough to fit three of me. I opened up my jacket and gasped as the frigid air moved in. Mona pulled half my jacket around her shoulders and snuggled up against my side.

She giggled as we jogged down the road, stuck together from the waist up. As long as we kept moving we'd be fine, and the faster we got to school the sooner we could warm up.

"You're late," the nun said, without looking up from the blackboard she was writing on.

I shuffled Mona to her desk, leaving the jacket on her—it wasn't that warm in here—and quickly slipped into my own desk on the other side of the room with the boys. My older brother shot me a warning glance as if to tell me the nun was in a bad mood today. My insides quivered. I knew it was my turn to lead the Lord's Prayer.

"Art," she said, her voice sharp like a whip, "since you insisted on delaying our lessons this morning, I trust you won't delay us any further when you lead us in prayer."

A few giggles erupted around the class and I felt my shoulder's sag. I hadn't wanted to be late but my chores had taken longer this morning—they always did when I had to break the ice in the well to water the cattle and horses—and everybody knew I took forever to say the Lord's Prayer because of my terrible stutter.

The nun rapped on her desk with a ruler and I jumped. "Quiet class," she looked over at me. "Well?"

I stood quickly nearly knocking my desk over and another set of giggles erupted. I hated speaking publicly and everyone knew it. I cleared my throat but my stomach was so tense I felt sick. I wished I had had more to eat than just the toast this morning.

"N-n-n," I tried to push the word out but I just kept stumbling over it! "N-not-re P-p-pere…" the class laughed and I heard my brother giggle with his friends behind me. I struggled painfully through the prayer and when I finished I sat down and scowled, shoving the boy beside me as he mocked my stutter. I hated school and I couldn't wait to be done with it.

The school day was nearly done when the nun rapped on her desk again, "Children, when you are finished your assignments you may have the last hour to read."

That was a treat! We rarely got free time to read what we wanted to. There was a small shelf in the corner that held books and, although I couldn't read, there was one book there that I loved. The nun had read it to us once and ever since then whenever we had time to read I would choose that book.

"Hey!" I nudged my cousin's shin with my boot.

"What?" He hissed at me.

"Will you read me that book I like?"

"Sure," he shrugged, "go get it."

I went to the bookshelf at the back of the room and scanned the covers looking for the one I wanted. The book was called 'Dominique' It was about a boy who loved the Lord. The boy would talk to God, all alone, and it fascinated me. His mom would go looking for him and would find him in his room talking to the Lord. Something in me was drawn to that idea. I wanted to be like Dominique—talking to God like I knew him—like he listened to me.

That night before bed, my siblings and I knelt to say our prayers. Mom set out the Virgin Mary and held the rosary beads and Dad knelt and clutched the crucifix.

"Hail Mary, full of grace, the Lord is with thee. Blessed art thou among women, and blessed is the fruit of thy womb, Jesus. Holy Mary, Mother of God, pray for us sinners, now and at the hour of our death. Amen."

We made the sign of the cross and mumbled the prayer along with our mother. I shifted from knee to knee and moved my lips, pretending to say the words, knowing I'd just stutter if I actually said them. I watched my mother carefully, how she spoke the prayer, how she bowed her head and scrunched her eyes shut—I imagined maybe she would be a saint one day—she certainly prayed enough to be one.

A candle sputtered noisily near the statue of Mary and I watched it cast shadows across the room. A fire glowed in the wood stove and even though the wind howled outside, I felt warm.

"Our Father which art in heaven," my Mom continued the rosary, her fingers diligently moving over the beads as she prayed. "Hallowed be thy name." I closed my eyes and waited for the prayer to be over.

"Art!" My brother kicked my back and shoved me over. "Move over!"

We slept in a huddled mass on the floor, tangled together to keep warm. I had an old jacket wrapped tightly around my shoulders so I wouldn't lose it to one of my brothers in my sleep. Already I could feel my toes tingling with cold and I pulled my legs up tight against my chest, trying to keep all the heat I could inside me. My brother Joseph tugged at the jacket trying to cover his legs and eventually he wiggled deep enough into the mix of us that he got warm. Slowly we settled into sleep, and as I heard the snores begin to rise around me I sighed and turned to the wall.

"Lord," I whispered, staring into the darkness, "if you hear me, I feel so lonely. I don't fit here. I'm stupid, I can't talk good, and nobody likes me." Saying the words out loud felt somehow better. Nobody listened to me when I talked but when I would talk to the Lord, somehow I felt he really listened, just like he listened to Dominique. "I wish I didn't stutter like I do," I whispered, "then maybe people would listen to me." I sighed and fell asleep.

CHAPTER TWO

# THE END OF THE STUTTER

It was early summer now and hot. Mom was cooking over the wood stove in the kitchen, sweat dripping off her nose, and my sisters were busy kneading dough and taking care of the little ones.

"Art!" Mom called to me. "Go tell Papa lunch is ready."

My dad would be working on the barn with the older boys plastering the cracks in the wood to get it ready for winter. I took off running. "P-p-papa!" I shouted, crossing the short distance to the barn.

My Dad saw me running.

"What do you want?" He asked.

I saw him swat one of my brothers and chuckle. "Let's see how long it takes him to spit it out."

I gulped, "M-m-mama s-s-says l-l-lunch…"

I heard panting behind me and knew it was probably my sister Mona.

"L-l-lunch," I said again, trying to hurry now.

"Lunch is ready Papa!" Mona's little voice chirped from behind me and my Dad laughed.

"Wow, Art, Mona's slow as a turtle and she got here and told me lunch is ready before you could f-f-finish your s-s-sentence." He mocked me. My brothers laughed at me as they walked back to the house.

I scuffed my toes in the dirt as I walked slowly back to the house. How could I fix this horrible stutter? It was then that a very clear thought came to my mind. Say one sound. Stop. Don't repeat it. Move to the next sound.

I stopped in my tracks. My mind was spinning, I suddenly had a clear picture of what I needed to do. "Not-" I whispered the sound, "tre pere." "Not—repere." "Notre pere." I said it out loud and felt a smile stretch across my lips. If I could say that first sound of a word without repeating it, I would be ok! I just needed to stop and take my time. "Not- RePere. Qui. Es. Aux. Cieux." This would take practice, but I was sure I could do this now! I'd be speaking without a stutter in no time.

When we went back to school that fall I felt confident for maybe the first time in my life. I knew when the nun asked me to say the Lord's Prayer that I would be ready this time.

It didn't take long for my turn to come around.

"Art, it's your turn to lead us in prayer," the nun said, and she waited expectantly for me to begin.

I rose smoothly to my feet and the rest of the class joined me. We always had to stand when we prayed the Lord's Prayer. I felt a small flutter of nerves in my stomach but I easily pushed them aside and focused. Just one sound, then stops. I told myself. Don't repeat the sounds. I cleared my throat and began, "Not-re Pere qie es aux cieux…"

I had done it! I felt a glow fill me as I finished. No one laughed—no one spoke—the room was quiet. I sat down and bowed my head shyly, waiting for the others to sit and the class to begin.

I never stuttered again during those school prayers, and soon my stutter was gone altogether.

CHAPTER THREE

# THE POWER OF PRAYER

My mother was a praying woman and I always believed God had mercy on me because of my mother's prayers. My earliest memories of my mom are of her on her knees urgently praying to God. She was a devout Catholic and her life was hard but she always had a desire to please God.

I came home from school one day looking for my sister Mona. We usually walked home together, but today she hadn't been there. I entered the house and looked through the shadowy light to find her curled up, a ragged sweater wrapped around her shoulders. She had wedged herself next to the chimney pipe to get as warm as possible but she was shivering.

"Mona?" I said, coming closer to look at her. "Are you alright?"

Her eyes barely opened as she looked at me. I felt scared when I saw her—her face was bright red and splotchy with fever.

"Go get Maman," she said in a scratchy voice. Her lips were dry and peeling. I ran to find my mom in the kitchen.

"Maman!" I shouted, "Come quick! Mona is sick."

Mom looked at me sternly because I was usually up to no good—trying to steal food from the kitchen or get in some other mischief—but today she could tell I was worried. She wiped her hands on her apron and quickly followed me to the girls' room.

"Mona?" She rushed to Mona's side and felt her face with the back of her hand. "My God, you're burning hot!" She scooped Mona up, away from the chimney, and laid her on the mattress that was usually reserved for the older girls. Mona was shivering.

"Art, get your father's blanket and bring a bucket of water and a rag from the kitchen!" Mom barked at me.

I ran.

When I got back with the blanket my mom tucked it all around Mona, then dipped a rag in the cold water and put it on her forehead. "I'm so cold, Maman," Mona said. I climbed up onto the mattress by Mona's feet and sat on them to try and warm them. Maman was whispering soothing words to Mona, but I couldn't hear them. I was very worried. What if Mona would die?

We sat that way for a while, and my mom did not leave Mona's side.

"Maman, I'm dying," Mona said.

"Don't say such things!" Mom scolded.

I went to stand beside Mona. Her eyes followed me. "Don't worry about me," she said, a faint smile on her lips. Her eyes closed.

"Look," she said, "I can see my body down there…"

My mom screamed, she dropped to her knees and cried to the Lord in desperation, and as she cried unto the Lord it seemed like a bright light embraced her.

"Don't take my child!" she cried.

I backed out of the room silently. I didn't want Mona to die.

I didn't know what to do with these feelings inside me. I went outside to sit on the steps and to wait.

I only went back inside when I heard Maman bustling about in the kitchen again. I entered cautiously. "Maman?" I asked, my eyes big with fear.

"She's asleep," Mom nodded without looking at me. "Leave her rest."

I felt a giant weight lift off of me. She was ok!

Mona slept all that night, and the next morning I rushed to Mona before anyone was up. I had chores to do, but I wanted to make sure she was still there. I crept into the room and Mona was just sitting up from her sleep. She looked at me and smiled.

"Art!" She said. "You shouldn't be in here!"

"Shh!" I hushed her. "You're ok!"

"Oh yes!" she smiled again, "I feel good!" Her face was no longer red and her eyes looked bright again. I felt relieved.

"Good!" I left the room quickly and Mona followed right behind me.

"Mona!" I heard my mother's voice and jumped. She was just coming into the kitchen to start the stove. "Get back to bed!" she scolded Mona.

Mona scowled, "I feel better, Maman!"

"To bed with you!" Mom shooed her off.

Mona looked over her shoulder at me and sulked back into her room.

I went into the barn to do my chores, but I peered out the barn door a few minutes later and saw Mona pulling her sweater on and sneaking out of the house. She was heading for the bush to check her rabbit traps.

Just before breakfast, about an hour later, we were all about to sit at the table when Mona walked in, bright and cheery. "Look, Maman!" She held a rabbit in each hand. "I caught these rabbits in my traps!"

Mona had been healed. Not a trace of the sickness remained.

Many years later Mona was getting blood work done at the Doctor's office.

"I don't believe this," the doctor said, "your blood work shows evidence that you've had scarlet fever."

Mona nodded, thinking back to that time she had been so sick.

"How was it treated?" the doctor asked.

There was no cure back then!

"God healed me!" she replied.

Was it because of my mother's prayers? Had God looked down on my dying sister and decided to give her back her spirit? I didn't know the answers, but at such a young age, I knew the miracle was a testament to the power of prayer. I saw my mother cry out to God and somehow my sister lived. It gave me hope that perhaps God could hear my prayers too.

CHAPTER FOUR

## TELL MY MOM!

I always felt like I didn't fit in with my family. Maybe it was because I was the middle child of so many, or maybe because of my stutter as a young child, but often I would hear my siblings talk about me. They would call me names, and once when I was very little I heard my older brother ask my mom, "Maman, why do you hate Art?"

I was only two or three years old, but I knew that my mom did not like me. I felt rejected. I felt repulsive even. So young and I already wondered why I had been born. Why had my parents had me, if only to hate me? Maybe that is why I loved the Lord. The idea that there was a God who loved me just as I was, was something beautiful and unfathomable to me, but I wanted desperately to believe it.

As a very young boy I would sing songs to God: little made up songs, about how much I loved him. I would talk to him as if he were right there with me, as if he were attentive to my every thought and word.

One day something very terrible happened to me. I won't go into the details, but in a family as big as mine, some weird things happened, and I don't think it happened just to me. I was hurt by one of my older sisters and, when I tried to tell my mom about it, my sister told my mom I was lying and that I had done something very bad and dirty.

My mom was overtaken with fury. She hated me already. Everyone knew that, so when my sister told her that lie, she acted without any hesitation. She dragged me down to the woodshed, grabbed a big heavy stick, and started to hit me. She beat me across the bones of my arms so hard I can still feel the pain to this day. I couldn't understand her hatred and her fury. I couldn't understand why my sister had said those things about me. I felt sick when I saw the look in my mother's eyes though, as if she were disgusted by me. When she was done, she turned and left me there by the woodpile.

I crawled behind the wood, clutching my throbbing arms to my chest, and cried.

"God," I felt the tears stream down my dirty cheeks, "you know I didn't do it. I know I didn't do it, but my mom doesn't know." The cries were coming so deep from inside me I felt my chest heaving for air. "Can you tell my mom I didn't do it? I don't want her to hate me." I sat there long into the evening, my small body beginning to shudder as the night air crept in.

Finally, I stood shakily and made my way back into the house. Supper was over, but for once I wasn't hungry. I climbed up into the loft and slumped down beside my brothers, most of whom were already asleep.

"Are you ok?" I heard Norbert whisper to me.

"Yeah." I whispered back.

Norbert nodded and let me move in closer to get warm.

"It'll be better tomorrow, you'll see."

I nodded feeling the pain radiate down my arms right into the bones. I wanted to cry some more but I had no tears left to cry. Please tell my mom I didn't do it, I prayed to God one last time as I drifted off to sleep.

My mom did apologize to me but it was much later in life. She struggled with her feelings towards me—something in her hated me—yet she loved the Lord. I'd seen the evidence in her prayers. I don't always understand God's ways, but I know that my mom did the best she could, and I love her for it.

CHAPTER FIVE

# EARNING GRACE

Norbert sat beside me and giggled as I carefully wound a rubber band between my fingers, slipped a folded up paper into it, and stretched it back as far as it would go. I looked over at him and winked, then let the paper fly. It hit a girl across the room right in the cheek and she screeched.

I quickly ducked my head and pretended to be practicing my arithmetic assignment.

Sister Theresa didn't even have to ask what had happened, I felt her sharp eyes scowling at me from the front of the room. "Who's launching paper at the girls?" she asked, her eyes never leaving my bowed head.

No one spoke but a few boys snickered in the front.

"Art," Sister Theresa walked slowly to my desk, "I'll need your help weeding the grotto after school today."

I lifted my head to protest. I had chores to do after school.

"Chores can wait," she said, knowing full well how my dad felt about us being kept after school. "I sense you could use some grace, and weeding the grotto earns grace from Mother Mary."

"Yes, Sister Theresa," I sighed and glanced over at the girl I'd hit with the paper. She was rubbing her cheek and sulking. Norbert kicked my shin and grinned at me and I smiled back. It had been worth it.

I had to weed the grotto for two whole hours after school that day before Sister Theresa was satisfied. I was starving as I set off to walk home, where I knew my dad would be angry and my mom would probably not have saved any supper for me. I stopped by my uncle's store to try to beg a small snack off of him. Maybe he'd give me a cookie or some nuts.

I pushed open the door and heard the familiar bell jingle. My uncle looked up from behind his shop counter. I saw his eyes narrow. "What are you doing here this late?" He asked.

I rubbed my stomach and admired the display of candy on the counter top. "Sister Theresa had me weed the grotto," I said. "And I'm starved. Could you spare me some nuts?"

"Sure, if you've got the money."

"How about this?" I said. "Sister Theresa said I earned grace today. I'll give you half my grace for a chocolate bar."

My uncle laughed at me and shook his head. "You kids are something else. Get on out of here, Art, and get home to your dad or you'll be needing more than grace when he's done with you."

I slouched back out the door and headed home, dragging my feet. What was the point of grace if it couldn't get you anything? I must have had a lot stored up by now. I'd been working lots of chores for Sister Theresa and the other nuns.

There was a field day coming up at school and that day was always exciting. There would be lots of tables set up where people would be selling goods and the money would go to the church. The nuns were always generous on those days as they usually reaped a fair amount of money for the church.

I knew if ever there was a chance for me to cash in my grace, it was now.

"Sister Theresa?" I approached her the morning of the field day.

She looked up, surprised. I usually didn't seek out attention from her.

"Yes, Art? What can I do for you?"

"Well," I thought carefully about how to word this. I had been planning for several days now and I didn't want to blow it, "I've been working an awful lot over the past few years, for the Sisters and the church, and I've never asked for a penny." That was true—though I'd certainly thought about it—I'd never asked for money. She narrowed her eyes and watched me continue. "And I was just wondering, since today all the money goes to the church anyway, if you could give me some money?"

I watched in disbelief as her hand reached toward the small purse she kept with coins. "I've been planning to give you children some spending money today anyway," she said. She pulled a dollar from the purse. "And you certainly have been working hard—although that never goes unpaid you know—what you don't make in money you make in grace."

I smiled anxiously, waiting for the precious dollar to be placed in my hand. She hesitated for a moment, her hand hovering over mine. Then I felt my fist close over the dollar and I knew I'd done it! The money was mine!

"Thank you Sister Theresa!" I smiled glowingly at her and ran off to join the field day activities.

I had no intention of spending that money. I knew the value of it. It was far more valuable than anything I could get here. Whether I was hungry or not, I wasn't going to let even one cent of that dollar leave my hand.

Sister Theresa came up alongside me several times throughout the day, encouraging me to buy things. "Look at this pail of buttons, Art, a whole pail of them for just fifty cents!" I pretended to look interested and search through the buttons.

"Wow," I said. "So many different ones, what would I do with them all?" I looked down at the ragged shirt I was wearing—I was quite sure that all my siblings and I combined wouldn't have enough clothes to use even a handful of those buttons on.

"Well!" She looked flustered. "There's a lady selling cookies. Perhaps you'd like some of those?"

I shrugged. "Sure I'll go have a look." Then I disappeared

around the school house until she was off my tail again.

I knew already at this young age that without money, you couldn't do anything in life. I'd keep that dollar and get some more too, until I had enough so that maybe I could move to the city and get a real job. I was only ten, but I had ambition in me not matched by many. I knew I couldn't stay here—I didn't belong—and this dollar was the first step towards my freedom.

CHAPTER SIX

# LEAVING HOME

By the time I turned fifteen, I was far from the little boy who swung on the swings and sang songs to God. I was focused on survival now—just making it out of this place alive. Things were tense at home. Money was tight, as usual, and there were nineteen kids now.

Usually when we turned sixteen Dad would kick us out with nothing more than the clothes on our backs. I knew my time was fast approaching. I was useless in school. What was the point of even trying anymore? The nuns wouldn't move me past grade two and I still couldn't read or write well. I was a fifteen year old boy sitting with little kids trying to do the same work they were doing and I felt like a fool. Eventually I stopped bringing my books to school with me.

"You better bring your books," my Dad said to me, "or I'll beat you every day until you do."

"Start now," I said, jutting out my chin. "We might as well get a head start because I'm not bringing them to school. Not now, not ever."

It wasn't more than a few days later Dad threw me out the door. "You're a stubborn ass," he said, cuffing my head. "Get out and don't come back."

The sky was pitch black—there were no street lights in this small town—and I could barely make out the road in front of me. I knew there was a small hunting shack in the bush not far away, and I made off in that direction. The shack was long abandoned. We'd all heard rumours a body had been found dead there, and I didn't relish the idea of spending any sort of time there, never mind sleeping there!

I focused on just walking, taking one step after the next and tried to quiet my raging mind. What was I going to do? Where was I going to go? How would I eat? How would I ever make it out of this place alive? Would anyone even care if I died?

"God," I whispered into the night, I hadn't spoken to God in a very long time. "I don't want to die here." The words drifted off my lips and into the darkness. I lay there and shivered all night long, waiting for morning.

CHAPTER SEVEN

# HOMELESS

"Hey!" Someone banged on the car window and I instantly jumped up. "Get out of there!"

I was out the door before they had finished the sentence.

The cold wind hit me as I ran down the frosty Winnipeg streets, breathing puffs of white into the black air. I could hear the footsteps of the man chasing me but I knew he wouldn't catch me.

I hopped over a fence into someone's yard and kept running, jumping and loping over bushes like the deer I'd seen so often growing up in St. Labre. I stopped when I knew I'd lost the man and bent over to catch my breath.

I patted the pockets of my dirty and worn jeans to make sure I still had my money. I had added the twelve dollars I'd made yesterday (piling tires at the stockyard in St. Boniface) to my small cash roll. I was starving, but I knew I had to save every dollar I could if I wanted to get enough for rent.

I'd been sleeping in cars for a few weeks now and it was exhausting. I'd work twelve hour days at the stockyard, rolling and stacking old tires. Then I'd walk the streets waiting for people to go to bed so I could find a car to sleep in for the night. It was getting cold and winter would be here soon. I knew I couldn't do this forever. I had to find a place to stay soon or I wasn't going to make it.

I straightened up and cast my eyes around the street looking for any sign of the man who had been chasing me but he was nowhere in sight. I rubbed the back of my neck, sore from the kinked position I had been in the car. Maybe I could find a bigger one to sleep in the rest of the night if I was lucky. I shoved my cold hands into my pockets and began walking down the street again, checking each car as I went for unlocked doors.

At last I found one that was open. I curled up in the back seat and tried to still my beating heart. I felt so alone, so empty inside, and so full of pain. I had nobody I could turn to for help, nobody I could rely on and, most of all, nobody who cared whether I lived or died. My soul cried out inside of me. It ached with a desire I had no way to fulfil. Something was missing in my life and I didn't know who or what it was but I knew I needed it desperately.

CHAPTER EIGHT

## MEETING LORRAINE

I began to start renting rooms when the weather turned cold. It would usually just be a bed in someone's house or a dorm room of sorts—whatever was the cheapest thing I could find. I didn't have a car yet, so I never really got out to see my family, but I worked hard and saved my money, every scrap I could, looking forward to the day when I could finally have the freedom to do what I wanted.

My brothers would come visit sometimes and we would help each other out whenever we knew work was needed somewhere. We were all experienced bush workers (our father had given us that much), so it was easy to get hired out whenever a company needed extra workers for short jobs here and there. My brothers were a crazy lot. Tough, loud, and French—we always drew attention wherever we went. Even though we were all out of the house now, I still didn't feel like I fit in.

They were rough with women and lousy with money and I hated seeing that in them. I didn't want to be like that. I liked the attention I got from women—there was plenty of it—but I could never stomach the idea of treating them badly. I didn't like going to bars. It was a waste of money, but once in a while my brothers and I would pile into a car and drive out to Woodbridge for the town dances. It felt good to show up there clean and well groomed. My mom would scowl at me and warn me, "Don't chase after the girls, Art." But I never had to. The girls chased after me!

I'd always been told I was ugly—I thought people would be

repulsed by me—but I knew now from my experience that people generally liked me when they met me. And girls! They seemed to really like me.

At first I thought what's wrong with them? How come they like an ugly guy? But I began to realize slowly that maybe I wasn't ugly after all. I might have even been good looking.

My brothers would be arguing over who would get what girl at the dance, but Norbert would just laugh at them. "You're not getting anybody," he'd say. "Art's coming to the dance." And it was true! The girls all liked to dance with me.

I was eighteen when I met Lorraine. She lived in Winnipeg, not far from where I worked, and she made it happen that we ran into each other pretty often. We started dating shortly after we met. She was my first real girlfriend and I wanted to treat her right, but I knew I wasn't ready for marriage or anything serious yet—I was just discovering my life! There was so much I still wanted to do.

I got a phone call one day from Lorraine's mom, telling me to come over, they wanted to talk to me. I knew from the phone call that it was serious.

I got to Lorraine's place after work that evening and her mom met me at the door.

"Come sit down," she said.

I entered the living room and joined Lorraine, who was already sitting on the sofa. I felt nervous and out of place with her mom there.

"What's going on?" I asked.

Lorraine wouldn't look at me.

Her mom sat down in front of us. "Lorraine is pregnant," she said. "And I've got no doubt who the father is."

The words hit me hard. I looked over at Lorraine, shocked. "Is it true?"

She nodded. "We saw the Doctor today to confirm."

"Now you listen here," her mom said, pointing at me. "I will not have my daughter's reputation smeared. Lorraine is a good girl and she comes from a good family, and we intend to keep it that way."

Her dark eyes squinted at me. "You're young and you've had a hard life, but now it's time for you to grow up. You'll marry my Lorraine. It's the right thing to do."

Marriage? I was too young to be married. I had barely begun my life and now I was going to be a father? How could I? I didn't know the slightest thing about being a dad. And although Lorraine was my girlfriend, I certainly wasn't ready to marry her.

"I can't," I said at last. "I don't even have a place for us to live."

Lorraine's mom crossed her arms and frowned. "You can live here with us until you find a place of your own."

Marry Lorraine and then move in with her mom? It was too much.

Her mom must have seen my resolve forming. "If you have any plans on seeing your child, you will marry Lorraine," she threatened.

My child. I could decide what I wanted about Lorraine and her mom, but I couldn't change the fact that Lorraine was going to have my baby, and I knew I could never abandon my child.

"We'll take care of the wedding," Lorraine's mom was saying, "but I promise you, you will never see that child if you don't marry Lorraine."

My whole world had been turned upside down from this discovery. I couldn't think straight, I felt shaky and confused, but the one thing I knew was that I wanted to be in my child's life.

"Make the wedding," I said. "And I'll show up."


Finding out I was going to be a husband and a father all at the same time hit me harder than I could have imagined. I sat down alone in my room that night and tried to picture me raising a family.

I already knew I would never let my child grow up hungry like I had. I was going to provide everything I could for Lorraine and the baby.

Still, I felt empty inside. As a child, I had at least held the hope of getting out of my house, getting money and being free. But now I was going to have a family of my own to look after. I could feel anxiety creep in but I pushed it down deep inside of me. I would get through this.

## CHAPTER NINE

## A FATHER'S LOVE

This day that my son was born, I knew my life was forever changed. Holding that tiny boy close—my own child, a piece of me—I had a small glimpse of what it felt like to be a father. The feelings that overtook me were unlike anything I had ever experienced. Until now, my life had always been about me: what I wanted to do and how I was going to do it. Suddenly all that had changed. I looked down at Darren and felt my world tip on its axis.

I had no experience to draw on. No wisdom to grab hold of. My relationship with my own father was nothing to speak of. There was such a void in me, a gaping hole I didn't know how to cross. How did I get from childhood and this overwhelming poverty to becoming the man, father, and husband I wanted so desperately to be?

How could my own parents have left me so unprepared for this life? Who would teach me how to be a father?

I clutched my son close and traced his tiny face with my own rough fingers.

I didn't yet know the love of a father, but soon I was about to encounter my own true Father, and that would forever change my life.

CHAPTER TEN

## GOD, ARE YOU REAL?

It was cool outside and sunny, the kind of spring morning that makes you think winter has had its last touch on the land and, although the ground was still brown and muddy, the sky was a startlingly clear blue.

I was working with a construction company at the University of Manitoba and was down in the bottom of a pit that had been dug out to begin pouring concrete for the foundation. It was hot, dirty, hard work—using a shovel to dig holes in the trenches for pipes to go through. I hadn't been in this pit for more than an hour but already I was sweaty and covered in mud. I was used to hard work, anyone would know that by looking at me, but today I was miserable, frustrated with life and the responsibilities I carried. I felt trapped, working all my life and never moving forward. I had such a yearning for more in life, but I never seemed to be able to get there. I stopped for a moment to wipe the sweat from my face and neck. Lifting my eyes to the clear blue sky I felt myself thinking, What's the point?

At that moment I felt everything around me go still. It was as if someone had turned the volume down all around me, and it was just me there in the mud, when the Word of the Lord came to me, "You are going to work hard, die, then what?"

All around men scurried about. Heavy machinery whined and growled, jackhammers pounded through concrete, but I heard nothing but the beating of my own heart. A million thoughts ran through my mind. I didn't know whether to be terrified or excited. A memory surfaced of me as a child crying out to God. I used to do that. I used to believe that God cared—that he loved me somehow, and that he would help me—but I had lost that innocence a long time ago. Now I felt it again, a yearning for that missing piece in my life.

"God," I whispered it at first. Then lifted my head and said louder, more desperately than I'd ever said anything before, "God, are you real?" My hands clenched the shovel I held tightly as I grappled with the feeling inside of me. I stood trembling. "If you're not real then this is all there is and I'm no better than a dog. I'll just die and go into the ground." I looked up at the sky again. "But if you are real then there's more to my life than mud and hard work. There's life after I die."

All at once it was so clear. If God was real then I wanted him above all else!

I panicked. How could I find him?

"God, make yourself real to me!" I begged.

I looked around, suddenly aware of my surroundings. Nothing had changed. Work was still going on at full speed. The noise was almost deafening after the strange silence, I had just witnessed in that moment. Work hadn't changed, but I had changed.

God was real, he had spoken to me, and I needed to know him.

I got home from work that night physically and emotionally exhausted. Lorraine met me at the door with Darren in her arms. I scooped him up and held him close, leaning over to give Lorraine a kiss.

"How was work?" She asked.

I didn't answer right away, but set Darren down in his high chair.

"What's wrong?" She asked, sensing my distress.

"I heard something today at work… a voice." I said, knowing I sounded crazy. "God spoke to me."

She gave me a questioning look. "What are you talking about?"

"I was working in the mud and I heard God say to me, 'You're going to work hard, die, then what?'"

"People don't just hear God's voice like that do they? I mean…what are you saying?"

"I don't know! But I need to find out about God. If he's real Lorraine, how can I find him?"

Lorraine shrugged uneasily and busied herself putting supper on the table. "Why don't you just forget about it? You've been working really hard lately. Maybe you're just tired."

I could tell this conversation wasn't going anywhere. She didn't believe me, or if she did, she didn't really care.

I couldn't sleep that night. My mind was so busy trying to figure out how I was going to learn more about God. Who could I talk to? Who could teach me? I didn't even own a Bible, and if I had, I wouldn't have been able to read it. Never had my grade two education been such a disappointment to me.

CHAPTER ELEVEN

## CALL FOR HELP

For a long time I looked for people to talk to. I looked up anyone I could remember that seemed to me had been religious or claimed to know God. I just wanted to talk to them, to hear about God. But I couldn't find anyone. Most were uncomfortable with my questions and didn't have any answers for me. I knew one of my brothers claimed to be a Christian now, but he was living way up north and I had no way to talk to him! I asked my brothers about him, if they knew anything, but they wouldn't talk! Maybe they thought I would criticize him, I don't know, but all I got was silence.

It was while I was walking downtown one day that a face came to mind of a woman I knew was religious. I felt a strong urge to go to her house. Maybe she could help me. I found her door easily and I walked up to ring the bell.

I wonder what her thoughts were as she opened the door. She probably assumed I was a salesman of some sort, or maybe a Mormon, or Jehovah's Witness. Either way, she didn't seem surprised or threatened at the sight of me. "Yes?" She asked, her face open and friendly.

This is it, I thought, this lady can help me. "Do you know God?" It wasn't what I had planned to say, but then I hadn't really planned any of this at all.

She opened her door wider. "Why don't you come in?" She invited me into her kitchen, which was clean and tidy. "I do know

God," she began, offering me a place to sit. "What is it you would like to know?"

I didn't know where to begin. "How do you get to know God? What is he like?"

She smiled, "Oh, he is good. He feels so good." I stared at her, waiting for her to continue. She leaned forward, "What's the best thing you've ever tasted?"

That was easy. "Well, I really like a cheeseburger." Where I grew up food wasn't eaten for its taste: we ate to live, we didn't live to eat. And it's a good thing too because it never tasted very good. But when I first had a cheeseburger… well, there wasn't anything better. Just thinking about it now made my mouth water and I promised myself another one soon.

"Well, you know the feeling of tasting a cheeseburger and knowing you just want more?"

"Yes."

"God is like that. Once you taste him, once you experience him, you never forget it. You want more."

I liked that. It was how I felt. I had heard him speak and I wanted more of him. "How do I get more of God?"

"Ask God to forgive you of your sins. Tell him you want him in your life."

"That's it?"

"That's the start."

I stood up from her table, "Thank you. This has meant a lot to me."

"You're welcome anytime." She said, and walked me to the door.

Just like that it was done. God had led me here, I knew that much, and now I couldn't wait to get out and pray!

From what I knew growing up, people only prayed at night or at Mass. I had asked for forgiveness before too, but always because I'd been forced to in confession. I had never really felt like I had anything I had needed to confess and sometimes I had been tempted just to make stuff up to get it over with. But this time was different. I knew I was bad and I didn't deserve God's forgiveness, but I wanted it!

I wanted to be clean, and righteous, so that God could be in my life! I had such a longing for God. My sins were heavy on my heart and I was desperate for a change. If I couldn't have God, then I didn't want life either.

I glanced around the busy street to see if anyone was watching me. I didn't want to make a spectacle of myself, but I knew I couldn't wait until night to pray. I ducked into a shadowed alley between two houses. It was darker there and felt private, like my old place behind the woodpile.

I closed my eyes and I called to the Lord from my most inward being. I was desperate. "Lord, you spoke to me in the mud and I heard you. I tasted you, and I want more. Forgive me, Lord, I know I'm a bad person! But I want you in my life. Make yourself real to me and I will do anything you say!"

Something happened then, unlike anything I had ever felt before. Something deep inside of me came to life. It was like I had lived in darkness, my whole life and now someone had turned a light on! I had been burdened down and miserable and now I felt as light and as free as an eagle.

I walked away from the ally and by the time I hit 445 Kennedy Street I was a changed man. A new creature. I couldn't explain it, but I was bursting with life, with joy, with hope, with love. For the first time in my life I didn't feel dirty and unwanted. I felt clean, and desired.

God had come to me—Arthur Adam, a nothing and a nobody. He had heard my cry and come to my rescue. I had been looking for something all this time, but I didn't know what it was. Now I knew it was God.

CHAPTER TWELVE

## HELP OFFERED

After that moment when God first touched me, I began to experience something I had never imagined was possible. God's presence was with me. It was like he was right there with me in everything I did. When I was working, I felt him there. When I was at home with my family, I felt him there. As I searched for people to talk to, as I called out to him, he was always right there. He covered me and nurtured me like a Father does his child. I felt so loved and had such a sense of belonging. I was a brand new baby in the Lord and God was right there, leading and guiding me and hovering over me with his presence. I felt as if he were jealous over me—protecting me from the world. I would have so many questions, and I would talk to him, not like he was distant and far away in the heavens, but I talked to him as if he were right in front of me—and he was!

I was sitting at home one evening listening to the radio. I had found an evangelist I liked to listen to, Herbert W. Armstrong, and sometimes I would tune into his program and pretend I was the one giving the message. I would imitate his voice and imagine what it must feel like to preach a message over the radio or in front of a crowd. To think that as a child I had a stutter so bad I could barely talk and now I was imitating Armstrong flawlessly. "As old as the Bible is this story," he was saying, "Adam and Eve were placed in the garden..."

I had the volume low so that I wouldn't bother Lorraine, so I heard the phone ring and her pick it up.

"Hello?...He's not here right now—" she said, and I knew the call was for me. "...And I'd appreciate if you'd stop calling. He's not int—" I was up and taking the phone before she could finish.

"Hello?"

"Hello, Arthur?"

"This is Art, who's this?"

"My name is John. I'm a pastor here in Winnipeg and I heard about you from one of our members."

"Really? What did you hear?"

"I heard you were looking for answers, searching for God. I thought I would offer to help you. I could come see you and teach you the Bible. You could come to church too, of course."

"Okay, sure!"

"How about I come around tomorrow evening? We could do a Bible study."

I looked at Lorraine who stood with her arms crossed watching me. "Sure, come tomorrow." I hung up and turned to her.

"I don't like it Art. He's called several times and I think he's just being nosy."

"So let me deal with it then."

"My mom warned me about those people. They're holy rollers—climbing walls and shaking around on the floor like they're nuts."

"Do you see me rolling around on the floor?" I asked.

"It probably won't take long!" she crossed her arms. "Anyway, I don't want him coming here."

"I'll meet him somewhere else then."

"Fine."

"Fine."

John knocked on our door promptly at seven. I ushered him out quickly before Lorraine could even see him.

"Your wife has been putting me off for quite some time," he said shaking my hand. "I'm glad I finally got to talk to you."

John was tall and slim with black hair, a mustache, and sharp brown eyes. He had a ready smile and a firm handshake and seemed excited about God. I liked him right away.

"Lorraine prefers if we don't meet at the apartment," I explained, "but I brought my Bible." I held up my brand new purchase. "And I thought we could just go somewhere else."

"Why sure," John said. "Why don't we go to my car?"

"Any place works for me," I said, following him out of the building. When I laid eyes on his car I began to have my doubts. It was a '53 Chevy, I knew that much, but the rest was a mystery. Covered in rust, it was a pile of junk, barely keeping itself together. If we hit a pothole I didn't think we could recover.

"Does your church pay you to drive this?" I asked, opening the door and getting inside.

John just laughed, "No—this is what the good Lord gave us to drive and it's good enough for me."

John settled into the drivers seat. "So, where are you from Art?"

I grimaced, "Ever heard of St. Labre?"

"Nope."

"Well, that's where I'm from. A French town in the bush."

"So how'd you end up here in Winnipeg?"

I skipped the details. "I got a job here when I was sixteen and just decided to stay. There's not much work available where I'm from."

"I see." He turned to me. "Let's pray before we begin."

I quickly bowed my head and closed my eyes—it's what I assumed people did. But John lifted up his eyes heavenward and began to pray in a loud voice, like he was talking in front of a crowd and not just me. Then he switched languages and I felt my eyes grow big. I stared at him, then quickly looked around to see if anyone was watching. What was coming out of his mouth was no language I'd ever heard. It must be tongues. I'd never seen anyone speak tongues before.

Then he said, "Amen," and I quickly looked away and pretended

I had had my eyes closed.

He fixed me with his piercing gaze. "So, are you saved, Art?"

"From what?" I asked.

"From sin. Are you born again? Has the holy spirit come into your life?"

"Well, I'll tell you what," I said. "I was nothing and nowhere and God spoke to me in the mud and I knew I wanted more. I called on God and he heard me! I know he did because I can feel him right here with me. I'm a changed man now. So yes, I guess I am born again. If that's what being born again is."

John was smiling and nodding. "Praise the Lord," he said. "Praise the Lord." He reached for his Bible. "Have you started reading the Bible yet? I always recommend starting with the book of John."

I ducked my head. "Actually, I can't read very well. I was hoping you could read and then I would follow along."

Knowing that I couldn't read didn't bother John at all, "Sure." He opened his Bible and flipped to John. I can't explain the feeling that came over me as I opened my Bible and searched clumsily for John. It was excitement, and hunger, and anticipation. I couldn't wait to learn more about God.

CHAPTER THIRTEEN

## SPEAKING IN TONGUES

When Sunday morning rolled around I started to feel nervous. I hadn't ever been to church before—not this kind of church anyway—just mass as a child and I knew this wasn't going to be the same. John had told me a lot about his church already and he had warned me it wouldn't be what I was used to.

I hadn't been a believer long, but already John was talking to me about joining the church, the need to be filled with the Holy Ghost, and speaking in tongues. I had heard stories about the holy rollers, similar to what Lorraine had said, where people were rolling on the floor and babbling, but I didn't know what to think. Maybe I would see some of that in this church, and maybe I wouldn't, but either way I was going to go see what it was about.

I dressed up really nice that morning, in my best suit and tie, and spent extra long minutes in front of the bathroom mirror shaving and combing my hair just so. I wanted to fit in and not draw any attention to myself, but I also wanted to make a good impression!

I asked Lorraine if she wanted to go with me to church, but she just laughed.

Off I went, head back, shoulders straight, chin up, and my Bible tucked securely under my arm. I may not have felt confident, but I sure wanted to look it.

From the outside the building looked small. It was long and narrow with white stucco walls, a dark shingled roof and an overhang over the stairs leading up to the front doors. The front and the sides of the building were lined with narrow windows with coloured panes of glass. A large wooden cross was raised on a sort of pillar beside the front doors. As I mounted the concrete steps I tipped my head up to get a good look at it. Was this where I would spend the rest of my days as a Christian? I pushed through the front doors and was immediately struck by the noise.

Voices greeting each other, chatting, some were singing already, and there was a band playing at the front. John came up to me, a big smile on his face.

"Brother Art!" he said as he pulled me close and kissed me right on the lips! I backed up and looked at him strangely, repulsed. People were milling about everywhere, but no one seemed to notice the kissed greeting.

"It's just the Russian way," he explained. "I greet every man that way."

I felt uncomfortable about it, but I ended up just shrugging and moving on. I liked John, and eventually I came to expect his strange greeting—but it was hard for me to get used to!

People everywhere were shaking hands and saying, "Praise the Lord!" and "God is good!" I was used to the sort of hushed reverence of the Catholic church, so this was shocking—even more shocking than the kiss.

"Welcome brother," a man said, approaching me with a big smile. He stretched out his hand and I shook it, "You must be new here. Welcome, welcome."

"I'm Art," I said, "Art Adam."

"Welcome, Art," he smiled again. "Glad to have you here. Anyone who comes to praise the Lord is welcome here."

"Well, I sure have a lot to praise him for," I said.

"Head on into the sanctuary, Brother Art, service will be starting shortly."

I did as he said, moving through the people to make my way to a space in the back corner. The building was divided in two, with an aisle going down the middle and leading to a carpeted stage where a pulpit stood, situated in front of another giant wooden cross.

Everywhere I glanced I thought I saw people looking at me and they would just smile and nod, or give a little wave. It was impossible to hide here.

"Good morning," a loud voice said from the front. "It's good to be in the house of the Lord this morning, Amen?"

"Amen!"

I jumped as the whole congregation shouted the Amen.

"Brother Charles, come and lead us in worship this morning," the man invited. The man sitting behind the pulpit in a row of chairs on the stage came forward.

"Hallelujah!" someone shouted from the pew in front of me. That was echoed by other shouts throughout the assembly.

"Let's worship the Lord this morning," Brother Charles said. "Let's praise him in his sanctuary!" There were more shouts of praise from the people. "People of God—let's show the Lord how much we love him!" The music started up and immediately people were standing, clapping and swaying, stomping their feet and lifting their hands. Some were standing in the isles to have more room to dance and move around.

I didn't know the songs, but I did stand up—as uncomfortable as I was. I could see John and his wife in the front row, their hands raised in worship, and I wondered if I should do that too, but I didn't. A woman in the front started to jump around, shaking her head and shouting 'hallelujah' over and over again. The man beside me was quietly muttering in tongues. Throughout the assembly people were crying, shouting praises with their hands in the air, and speaking in tongues.

When Pastor John rose up to preach, his message was on the baptism of the holy ghost. I wondered if he was preaching to me, because I was new and wasn't speaking in tongues yet. But if tongues was the sure sign from God that you were saved, well, I wanted it. God was real to me and was doing things in my life and showing me things.

I wondered when I would start to speak in tongues.

## CHAPTER FOURTEEN

## DON'T RELY ON MAN

Growing up in St. Labre, Catholicism was all I had known. We were told it was the one true church. Now that I had met John he always emphasized that his church was the one true church. I was certainly learning the scriptures there—but whenever John wanted to talk about church doctrines I would lose interest. I didn't care who the founders were or what visions they may or may not have seen in order to found this church. I wanted God, plain and simple.

So when the Jehovah Witnesses found my door, I was surprised to hear, yet again, that their church was the one true church.

"Come in," I said to them, I was excited to tell them my testimony. "All my life I've been searching for God and I didn't know it," I said. "But then one day I was working in the mud and God spoke to me. He touched my life and I haven't been the same since."

I saw a spark of interest in their eyes, but it wasn't because of my testimony. They saw I was a new Christian and they had an opportunity to win me over to their faith. They began plastering me with doctrines backed up by scriptures that I knew nothing about. I was still brand new to the Bible.

"Would you mind coming back later this week?" I asked the two men. "I'd like you to meet with my pastor so we can discuss these things. I'm just new to the faith and would feel better if my pastor was here."

"That would be fine," they said.

I called up John and told him about the meeting. He agreed to come.

When the time came for the meeting, I was excited. When I opened the door to accept them back into my house, three Jehovah's Witnesses entered. John, who was already sitting at my table waiting, did not seem impressed. It turned out the two young men who had come by earlier had gotten their minister to come by for the meeting as well. I was certain John would do just fine.

It quickly became clear though, that the visitors knew their Bible very well. They were cool, calm, and collected, having answers and verses for everything John could throw at them, and John quickly became irritated and defensive.

When the men left, John looked at me as if I had betrayed him. He stood up and scowled, "If I had known it was going to be like this, Art, I never would have come."

"I didn't know it would be like that," I said, frowning. "I'm sorry."

I felt terrible.

John left, and I sat for a while at the table and stared down at my Bible in thought. I wasn't interested in anything I couldn't prove. Is this the kind of preacher I was going to be? Preaching to people about 'the truth' but having no proof of it? The thought disgusted me. I was reminded of a time as a child I had attended a catechism class for the Catholic church. We had been talking about Easter and I had asked the priest, "Why do they say Jesus was dead three days? If he died at 3PM on Good Friday and was raised on Easter Sunday morning—that's only about a day and a half!" The priest had become very mad and punished me for my 'insubordination'. But he had no answer for my question.

How was it that people could have such strong beliefs about things and yet not be able to back them up by the very Bible they claimed to believe?

Yet something had happened in that meeting. While both sides were arguing about a passage and what it meant, I felt God open the answer up to me. John was speaking on one side of me, but the Holy Spirit was speaking to the other, showing me the truth. I knew with an excitement and a certainty what the verses meant! And I knew God had shown it to me.

I began to see that maybe John didn't have all the answers. I had been placing my faith in a man—instead of God! Maybe God wanted to be my teacher. A hunger for truth and understanding overwhelmed me.

I went to my room and shut the door. It was dark, but there was a lamp beside my bed and the light fell in a pale circle on the floor. I dropped to my knees there in the lamplight and bowed before God. "Lord, I've got no education and I've been stupid my whole life." I took my Bible, opened it, and held it on top of my head, pressing it against my skull. "But if you open my mind—if you open your Word to me—I promise I will preach whatever you show me." The familiar feeling of God's presence stirred in me. I knew he would take care of me.

I was beginning to see that not everything I was being taught by John was accurate. I loved him, but I needed to test him. I didn't want him teaching me things that weren't true.

A few days later I was sitting in John's car and we were driving around town talking about the Lord when a question formed in my mind, and I knew God wanted me to ask it.

"John, where do we come from?" I asked.

"What do you mean, Art?"

"I mean were Adam and Eve the first people on Earth?"

"Everyone knows Adam was created first, then Eve—and through them came their first two sons Cain and Abel."

"Well," I paused, "how do we come to have so many people in the world, if there was only Adam and Eve and Cain and Abel? Did Cain have sex with his mother?" I was a straightforward guy and wanted truth above all, so I didn't mind being blunt.

John looked disgusted. "No!" He looked angry that I had asked the question—but what else was there to imply? "They had sisters…" he said lamely.

"Sisters? So is it ok then to have sex with sisters? Isn't that incest?"

The silence was deafening. He didn't have an answer. Here I was, an illiterate boy asking questions that made this learned man very nervous. I wanted to see if John had questioned the things he had been taught or if he had just believed them blindly. Now I had my answer. John could preach about what the church believed but he had never tested for himself what the Word of God had to say about those beliefs.

I would not depend on man for my learning anymore.

CHAPTER FIFTEEN

## QUESTIONS FOR THE PRIEST

Walking back into a Catholic church made me think of being a kid again. I felt like if I turned around my mom would be there herding me and my siblings into a hard wooden pew while my dad lazily made the sign of the cross and slouched in beside us. Today, though, this church was empty. It was mid afternoon in early summer and the sunlight streamed through a coloured window and I could see particles of dust hanging suspended in the light. The floorboards creaked as I walked down the center aisle and I stared at the large crucifix mounted on the wall high above the front altar. The cross loomed over me, displaying the pale and emaciated body of Jesus, his wounds bleeding and gaping, his face a mask of pain and sadness.

"Can I help you?" the voice came from behind me and I quickly turned to see the priest standing in his black garb with the white collar. "Did you need to make a confession?"

"Actually, I have some questions," I said, "but can we talk in your office?"

"Certainly."

He led me past a table of flickering prayer candles, past the statues of the saints with their offering boxes, and up onto the stage where a door stood partially hidden behind the crucified Jesus.

The priest offered me a chair and I sat.

"So," he leaned back in his own chair behind his desk and

looked at me. "Arthur Adam, am I right?"

"That's right," I said. He had married Lorraine and me less than two years ago.

"What can I do for you, Arthur?"

"I have some questions," I said, leaning forward, "that I want answers to."

The priest nodded for me to go ahead.

"Why have you lied to me? Why have you lied to my family?"

He looked startled, "What have I lied about?" He asked.

"My mom used to send money," I began, "for a dead person to get out of purgatory."

"That's right." He nodded. "It's a principal teaching within the Catholic church."

"Where in the Bible does it talk about purgatory? And even if there was a purgatory, why would you charge me to get me out of it? If this church caught on fire, I'd get you out of it. I wouldn't wait around for you to pay me! You claim to have power to save me from hell, but you won't do it unless I pay my dues."

He began to shuffle through some papers on his desk looking uselessly for something to back him up.

"And another thing," I said. "Why do you call Mary the 'Virgin Mary' after she had kids?"

"Well," he said, "she was a virgin—"

"Jesus had brothers and sisters," I cut him off. "She's not a virgin now, plain and simple."

He began to get angry at me, I could see by how red his face was. "You have a lot of nerve," he said. "Do you really think you are good enough to go to heaven?"

I shrugged. "Maybe heaven, maybe hell," I looked right at him, "but not purgatory where I sit and wait until you've got enough money in your pocket. And since we're talking about whether I'm good enough or not, my whole life I was taught to look to a man to forgive me my sins. Where do you get that power?"

He clenched his jaw. "The priest has all power to forgive sins."

"Show me the verse." I sat back.

He starred at me for a moment and finally reached for a Bible. It had dust on it.

There was no verse. I found in my life that too many people teach things they claim are in the Bible, but when asked for the verse they don't know it.

"The Bible says only God has the power to forgive sins," I said. I took the Bible from him and opened it to the verse 'who can forgive sins but God alone?'

"Is that all you have to say, young man?" He asked.

"Everything I was taught by this church," I said, "was a lie. God is not here. I was working in the mud when the Word of God came to me. He spoke to me—not through a priest, not through a saint, just Him to me. And I've never been the same. He's forgiven my sins—and he did it once, I don't have to keep asking. He's the one who controls my destiny and I don't have to pay a cent."

"I think it's time for you to leave." He stood up and so did I.

"I'll leave," I said, "but why would you lead a life that claims to worship God, yet nothing you teach is even in the Bible? You need Christ."

"Get out." He said, pointing to the door.

I left.

CHAPTER SIXTEEN

## PROFESSIONAL HELP

"You're turning into one of them, Art, a holy roller. My mom warned me about this." Lorraine said early one morning as we drank our coffee. I had been telling her about the things I had been learning about God.

"But is that a bad thing?" I asked, trying to keep my loud voice from waking our son. "If anything I've been treating you better than ever before."

"You treated me fine before. I never complained," She said. "You're not the man I married!"

"The man you married," I said, throwing my hands in the air. "Do you know how many pretty girls are at the University where I'm working? Do you think the old me wouldn't have done more than just look at them if I had the chance?" I felt my shoulders sag, "You should be happy I'm a Christian now! You've got nothing to worry about!"

"My mother called last night," she began.

"Oh great," I interjected.

She ignored me and continued. "She thinks you need help—professional help, Art." Her eyes met mine. "Would you be willing to see a psychiatrist?"

"If she thinks I need help so much, why doesn't she help me?" All my mother-in-law had ever done was speak against me. I wanted to do what was right, but I felt I always had a fight on my hands when Lorraine's mom got involved—which was often.

"You come from such a big family. You've suffered a lot as a child. Maybe you need more help than you realize dealing with it all."

I shook my head. "Well, I know she thinks I'm crazy," I said. "But do you actually think that?"

There was a moment of hesitation and that's all it took for me to know her answer. "Honestly, the way you talk now is just not normal. People don't hear God speak, Art, and I'm serious. I don't want to live with you anymore if you keep this up."

"You don't mean that."

"I do. And if it's alright with you I'd like to schedule an appointment with a psychiatrist."

"Fine." I pushed my chair back and stood up. "I'll meet with the Doctor. I just want what's best for us—for our family."

She got up and headed to the phone to make the appointment.

The appointment was scheduled for the next day, and Lorraine and my mother-in-law came in together with me.

"What is your name?" the psychiatrist asked, his pen poised over a fresh pad of paper. His glasses were perched on the tip of his nose and he looked at me expectantly over the rims.

"Arthur Adam," I said.

"When were you born, Arthur?"

"The first time or the second time?" I asked.

His pen paused and he pushed up his glasses to really get a look at me. "Do you mean to tell me you have been born twice?"

I could practically feel my wife biting her tongue beside me and my mother-in-law clasping her hands in smug satisfaction.

"Something happened to me and I call it a birth. I am a new person. My flesh hasn't changed but there is new life inside of me. " I spread my hands in emphasis.

"Hmm," I saw the Doctor glance at my mother in law, like she'd already warned him about me. "When did this 'new life' first begin for you Mr. Adam?"

"God spoke to me in the mud."

"God spoke to you," he repeated. I'm sure the doctor was delighted as he scribbled on his notepad. He probably thought he could make a lot of money off the many sessions he would need to straighten me out.

I leaned forward. "I heard the voice of God say to me 'you're going to work hard, die, then what?'"

"And what did that mean to you?" he looked up at me over his glasses.

"If God is real, then there's life or death. I knew I had to choose." I pointed right at him, "And I'll tell you something else. When you've been born once, you die once. But when you've been born twice you don't die at all."

The room was quiet.

The appointment was unproductive as it was clear I would not be swayed. We did not go back for a follow-up appointment.

## CHAPTER SEVENTEEN

# A FATHER'S BOND

Things in my marriage continued to get worse.

"That's it," Lorraine said one night when I came into the apartment after another meeting with John. "If you don't give up this ridiculous religion I'm leaving you."

Lorraine had been on the phone to her mom again. I knew she had been the instigator behind all this, but I just didn't understand why. I felt I had been nothing but respectful to Lorraine and kinder than I ever had been before. I truly wanted to make things work, but I knew I had to put God first.

"Do you hear what you're saying? It doesn't make any sense. I used to be so angry—ready to fight anyone for looking at me sideways. I'd let girls flirt with me, and like it too. Do you really want me to go back to that?" I asked.

"I liked you better the way you were. At least I knew you then. I knew what to expect. I don't know you anymore!"

"That's no reason to leave me at all and you know it," I said.

She remained silent, watching me.

"I will leave you," she said at last, "if you don't choose right now to give this up."

"I can't do that."

And there it was. She wanted me to choose between her, and God.

The next day I came home from work to an empty apartment.

Lorraine had taken Darren to her mother's and now the entire family had driven out from Yorkton, Saskatchewan to try to talk some sense into me before taking Lorraine back to Yorkton to stay with her grandmother. They called me over to the house to talk.

"Are you really going to let your wife leave you over a simple thing like religion?"

"You can't let something like religion get in the way of your marriage!" They said, as if I had a choice. I didn't though. There was no way now for me to turn my back on God and what he was doing in me.

"You have a family to think about," was their last argument.

But it was clear to me this wasn't just about religion. I may have only been twenty, but I was able to discern a lot about people. "If she is going to leave me because of my belief in God, she is going to leave me anyway." I said.

When the time came for the family to leave, Lorraine packed up her bags to go with them. I held Darren close as I walked them to the car outside. "I'll see you again soon." I whispered into his hair as I kissed him. My heart cried out to God as I placed my son into Lorraine's arms and watched them drive away. Why was this happening?

"God," I said, resting my head on the steering wheel. "I put you first, now you do something for me."

People say they put God first in their lives, but they don't even have a clue what that means.

John tried to comfort me at this time, but he didn't know what to tell me. In his church marriage was for life. The only way out was death.

"I'm praying for her, Art." John said that night, placing his hand on my shoulder. "That the good Lord will bring her back to you." Then, almost as an afterthought, he added, "You don't think she'll run around on you, do you?"

I shook my head. "You can stop praying for her to come back if she does!"

He seemed shocked. But I knew Lorraine wouldn't cheat on me. We loved each other—and although this was something we needed to work out in our relationship, we would work it out.

One night about a week later I got a phone call.
"Hello?"
"Hi Art," it was Lorraine.
I tried to keep my voice steady. "Hi! How are you? How's Darren?"
"We're good. Darren misses you," She paused. "Have you changed your mind yet?"
"I won't do that Lorraine. I can't. You already know that. But I love you! I want you to come back."
"What about God? Will you love me more than him?"
I shook my head, "God comes first, but I promise Lorraine, you're right next. You and Darren are both so important to me."
Again she was silent, she gave a big sigh, "Ok, come pick us up."
Yes! I jumped up. "I'm coming right now!"
It was a long drive to Yorkton but it went by quickly. I couldn't stop thinking how relieved I was that she and Darren were coming back home. Things would change now.
It was nearly two in the morning when I pulled up in front of Lorraine's grandmother's house and Lorraine was waiting for me inside.
"Hi!" I ran up the driveway and pulled her into a hug. She held on to me.
"I'm sorry," she whispered. Her apology wasn't much, but it was enough.
Then I saw him—little Darren had woken up and crawled out of his makeshift bed on the floor. He gave a sleepy grin and toddled towards me, his arms outstretched. I had tears in my eyes before I could stop them.
"Come here son," I reached for him and scooped him into my

arms. He wrapped his little arms around my neck and clung to me. "It's ok, Papa's here now." I patted him and held him as tight as I could without hurting him. He lay there against my chest and fell asleep, and I can't express how good it felt to feel his little body against mine again.

How is it a father can feel such love for his son?

All the way home I pondered the love of a father towards his son. I thought about my own feelings towards my dad, how he had never loved me, never held me close or made me feel safe and secure. Yet I couldn't think about Darren without being overwhelmed with feelings of pride and possessiveness. He was my son! I couldn't stand the thought that someone might try to hurt him or wouldn't protect him and take care of him.

And that was how God was to me. I had never had a father's love but I had called to God like he was my father. I depended on him. I needed his love and protection in the same way a child needs love and protection from a father. My own Papa may have beat me and called me worthless—but my heavenly father was jealous of me and paid a great price for me. To him I was priceless and his presence wrapped around me in a way that was more real than anything my earthly father could have done for me. Would I leave him? Never.

CHAPTER EIGHTEEN

## ALTER CALL

"So will you come to church with me this morning?" I asked. Lorraine had gotten up early and was wearing a nice dress. I didn't want to get my hopes up, but since she had come back home with me last week, she had changed.

"I thought I would come," she nodded. "I might as well get used to the fact that this is our new life now."

I smiled, "That's great!" We would be a family now, going to church together every Sunday. I couldn't wait for her to get to know the people at church, it would be nice for her to have some friends and be part of a community. Maybe God would touch her like he had touched me. I knew if God could touch a guy like me, he could touch anybody.

A few Sundays later John preached again about the importance of being filled with the Holy Ghost. Then he held an altar call.

Lorraine was the first one down the aisle. I wondered what her mother would think about *that*. I went down the aisle too, and knelt at the front. If God wanted me to speak in tongues, I knew he would do it for me. John came up behind me and began to pray in tongues over me. "Fill him with the Holy Ghost, Lord!" He continued the rest of the prayer in tongues.

I stayed there at the altar waiting for some time. People all around were falling on the floor, shaking, crying, and speaking in tongues. One man was on his knees banging on the pew and yelling. I glanced over at Lorraine, and there she was on the floor with the others, speaking in tongues and crying. I couldn't feel anything in me except confusion. Why didn't anything work for me? It seemed like everybody got the Spirit except me.

CHAPTER NINETEEN

# FEAR BANISHED

I was driving home from work one night when I felt struck with fear. Something or someone was in the car with me. I started thinking maybe there were demons in the car. I was almost paralyzed with fear. In my head, I started seeing visions of devils leering at me and I couldn't shake the feeling I was being watched, or worse. What if I was possessed? I quickly glanced over my shoulder into the back seat. Nothing. I should have felt relieved, but I didn't. I might not have seen anything but I was certain something evil was there.

At home I shut off the car and ran through the darkness as fast as I could into the apartment, leaving my lunch pail and jacket behind me. Did something just grab at my arm? I burst through the door into the light and warmth of the apartment and slammed it shut, leaning against it and breathing heavily.

Lorraine came to see what the commotion was about. She looked alarmed.

"Art? What in the world happened?"

"What? Oh, nothing, I just got home from work."

"Where's your lunch pail?"

"I must have forgotten it in the car, I'll go get it later." I distracted myself by picking up Darren who had run towards me, always happy to greet me at the door.

"How are you, my boy?" I asked him, throwing him into the air.

"Did you have a good day?"

"Yes!" he laughed. "Do it again, Papa!"

I tossed him into the air again.

"Careful, you might hit the ceiling!" Lorraine warned.

Our little apartment was too small, and I had wanted to buy us a house for a while now. I had finally saved up enough, and just in time too, because Lorraine was pregnant again. We would be moving next month into a house on Nassau Street. The house was simple, but bigger than this apartment, and it would have a nice backyard for the kids to play in.

"Ok, time to eat!" Lorraine brought a pot of stew to the table and set out a loaf of bread.

I was feeling better already, just being in the light, and the fear from the moment before was fading.

But the fear didn't leave.

For days, whenever I was alone the fear would haunt me. Finally, I cried out to God, and I heard him say to me, "I will set you free."

I knew it must have been Satan attacking me, because the minute God said that to me the fear was gone. That experience gave me confidence that God has total authority over Satan. Everyday I was learning new things about God and his plan for his people. I found out at a later time that fear is not of God. He has not given us a spirit of fear, but of a sound mind.

CHAPTER TWENTY

# MY BROTHER SET FREE

It was Sunday evening and I had invited one of my brothers to church. There were services in the morning and the evening on Sundays, but the evenings were usually when most of the action was. I knew my brother was doing drugs and he had lots of anger and fear in him. God had set me free from the attacks of Satan and I knew he could set my brother free too.

The service was in full force. The music was playing, John was at the front speaking and calling the people to worship. People were all over. It was loud. Suddenly my brother fell to the floor. His eyes looked wild and I knew it wasn't the Holy Ghost in him.

"Pastor John!" I called, "We need to pray for my brother to be set free!" It wasn't unusual for someone to fall on the floor during a meeting like this, but I knew inside me that my brother had spirits and it was the spirits that had made him fall on the floor. I knew God could set him free, but since I couldn't speak in tongues, I thought I didn't have the power to pray for him.

John came over and looked down at my brother. "What's the matter Art?"

Couldn't he see? It was so plain to me. "You need to ask God to set my brother free from spirits."

John seemed bothered, but he knelt beside my brother who was writhing on the floor, "Satan, come out of this man in Jesus' name."

I felt myself praying along. I knew God would do it.

Just like that, my brother stopped writhing. He lay still for a moment and then stood up. He was no longer crazy, but calm. "It's gone," he said and he looked at me. "I feel free!"

"Praise the Lord!" I said. "I knew he would do it for you!"

Pastor John said, "Praise God!"

## CHAPTER TWENTY-ONE

# BELONGING

We moved into our new house on Nassau Street in late fall. Over a year had passed since God had first touched me. Lorraine was pregnant with our second child and nearly ready to deliver. We had all the routes mapped out to the hospital and her overnight bag was packed and ready to go just in case. It was an exciting time for us.

John continued to come see me and do Bible studies with me. However, he stuck mainly to church doctrines. He treated me with respect and a sort of fatherly affection (something I hadn't had before) and in return he liked my youth and enthusiastic hunger for God's word. He considered me a good catch for his church and liked to talk about the Bible with me and be my teacher.

I had turned all my attention to learning about God. My mind was like a steel trap. I remembered everything I heard and before long I could recite it back. I was hungry to know everything.

Who was Jesus really? What was heaven like? Was there a rapture? Where was hell and who would go there? Everything I could think of I would ask John and he would point me to verses that were used to explain his beliefs. I felt almost as if God would come and read over my shoulder and show me things, things that John wouldn't show me. Almost like I could see into the verses and I would know they didn't always mean what John said they did. I would get so excited inside that I was learning and growing, and could feel the presence of God with me. I felt a desire to preach, and I knew that I would be preaching one day soon.

"Art, it's time we talk about you and Lorraine becoming members of our church," John said one evening during our Bible studies.

"Okay, what do I have to do?" I asked.

"Well, we can meet Sunday morning before church and go through the list of our doctrines. Then, in the church service, you and Lorraine would come up and publicly declare that you believe these doctrines and agree to follow them."

"Well, let's do it now!" I said. "Why wait a whole week?"

John scowled. "This is how it's always done," he said. "It's a big commitment, I'll let you two talk about it together and then we will make it official next Sunday."

"Okay," I shrugged.

I went home to tell Lorraine what had happened. She was in the living room waiting for me when I got home.

We hadn't been going to the church very long, but already she was a different person. She didn't wear makeup or jewelry anymore, and always wore plain clothes and hairstyles. She used to be a hair stylist when I first met her, interested in cosmetology and beauty products. So this was a big change! And she had made friends with a lot of other women in the church. She had become quite involved. They would always be having bake sales and fundraisers to raise money for the church.

"John wants us to become members of the church," I said to Lorraine, sitting on the couch beside her.

"What does that mean?" She asked, rubbing her back tiredly.

"Well, we have to agree with the church doctrines," I repeated what John had said to me. "And once we're members, we are really part of the one true church."

"Ok," Lorraine said.

"Will you sincerely promise in the presence of God and these witnesses that you will accept this Bible as the Word of God, believe and practice its teachings rightly divided—the New Testament as your rule of faith, practice, government, and discipline, and walk in the light to the best of your knowledge and ability?" John asked us in front of the congregation that following Sunday.

"We do," Lorraine and I said together.

"Yes!" Darren had come to the front with us and decided to chime in. Everyone laughed.

"Welcome to the Church of God, Brother Arthur Adam, and Sister Lorraine Adam and you, Brother Darren," John bent down to shake Darren's hand good-naturedly.

"Now we offer to you the right hand of fellowship. Let's pray a blessing over this family." John said a prayer over us and that was it. We were officially members of the church.

Two weeks later Lorraine delivered a beautiful baby girl.

When Darren was born, I thought I knew what it was like to be a father. I felt so proud of him, my son, a part of me. But when little Michelle was born something in me just melted. Dark curly hair and the brightest blue eyes you ever saw—like looking at the summer sky when there isn't a cloud in sight. Her tiny hand grasped my finger and held it close and instantly I knew there was nothing in the world I wouldn't do to protect her. She was a small piece of heaven that came down to us and brought joy everywhere she went.

I never took my children for granted. Maybe it was because of the way I was treated as a child—how desperately I had longed for attention from my parents—how I had longed to be loved—but whenever I could, I would hold my children close and love them. I was so proud of them. Michelle was only minutes old and I was already imagining what her future would be like. What I was going to do for her. How I was going to take care of her and provide all the opportunities I could for her and Darren.

CHAPTER TWENTY-TWO

# PREACHING

I was working in the bush with my brother clearing trees. It was just something I did part time to help him out when he needed it. I went to a secluded place in the bush where no one else was around and found an old moss covered stump. I stepped onto the stump and imagined a congregation in front of me. As the tall pine trees swayed in the breeze I began to recite a sermon I had heard on the radio.

"As old as the Bible is this story. Adam and Eve were placed in the garden of Eden and God said you can eat of every tree, except the one in the midst of the garden thou shalt not eat. So they had plenty. They didn't desire anything. They had everything they needed. God came down in the cool of the day and had communion and fellowship with them. But God told them there's something you're not supposed to have. Don't eat of the tree that's in the midst of the garden. But God did not make man as robots but God made man a free moral agent to choose to serve him..."

A breeze blew past me, the trees swayed and rustled. I could smell the deep scent of pine sap, dirt, and sawdust. I stepped off the stump and went back to work.

"Where were you?" My brother asked as I joined him at the worksite.

"Smoke break." I shrugged.

The next Sunday I asked John if I could preach.

"Do you have a message prepared?" John asked, somewhat surprised.

"Yes, 'You can get what you want, but you might not want what you get,'" I said proudly.

"Well," John scratched his head in thought, "I suppose I could give you some time this morning to preach, if that's what you want."

I grinned. "Thanks!" I felt nervous. I wanted to do this so badly.

John invited me to the front after the worship service. "Folks," he said into the microphone, "Brother Art has a message for us today. Let's welcome him."

There was a smattering of applause. I felt all eyes on me as I mounted the steps and found my way behind the pulpit. My heart was beating, my hands were sweating and my mouth was so dry I could barely swallow. I opened up my Bible and sat it on the pulpit in front of me. I wasn't going to use my Bible. I had everything memorized already, but nobody needed to know that.

I began, "As old as the Bible is this story. Adam and Eve were placed in the garden…"

I finished the message in record time and sat down at the back of the stage. John came up. "Thank you Brother Art. A wonderful message."

And it was. I felt proud. I knew it wasn't a message I had made myself, but it was a good message nevertheless, and couldn't it still be used to spread the word of God? I had at least five more messages just like that I had already memorized off the radio and TV. I resolved then that this would be just the beginning of my preaching.

I began to travel around after that, preaching at different churches and on reserves. I would preach the same message, or rotate different messages I had memorized from the radio and wherever I went people liked me. Every so often though someone would mention to me 'how interesting it is that you don't have an accent when you preach!' I would always smile and nod, but I knew it was because I was imitating other pastors and repeating the messages exactly as I had heard them.

## CHAPTER TWENTY-THREE

# I DON'T WANT TO BEG

It was time for the offering again. Pastor John was giving his weekly plea for more money for the church. It seemed every week there was another fundraiser going on. Church bake sales, craft sales, events—mostly things that the women handled. Lorraine was forever in the kitchen baking for the church these days, and the money it seemed we spent on baking ingredients was equal to our weekly tithes. Besides that, there would be an offering taken each service requesting money on top of what you were already giving. I was told over and over it is better to give than to receive.

Things had been tight for us lately, especially with the new baby and the new house. I was already working full time and picking up extra jobs everywhere I could, and still finding time to be fully involved in the church and outside evangelism. I had some friends now, Jerry and Earl. We would go out on weekends and preach and play music anywhere we could.

I opened up my wallet as the offering plate came my way. I only had a twenty dollar bill inside. I couldn't pass the plate without putting anything inside! I pulled the bill out of my wallet and tossed it into the offering plate. We would get by without it. Heck, I'd gone the first half of my life without ever seeing a twenty dollar bill. But I didn't want my life to be like it was growing up, always hungry, always worried about money. I wanted to be a good provider for my family and a good steward of what God had provided me with.

It was the Morris Stampede: loud, smelly, and hot. All around me people were walking by, girls chatting with their friends, mothers pushing strollers, groups of teens laughing loudly, families licking ice cream cones and busily moving from one vendor to the next. I was sitting on a dusty street curb watching the people go by. On the outside I looked just like a regular guy enjoying the day, but on the inside I was talking to God. I was praying for people as they passed, letting my inner man discern if there was someone here I should talk to. As I watched and waited, I began to think about the Earth, and how God, has dominion over everything and how he supplies everything.

I had been frustrated lately. There were big scandals happening on TV with different prominent Televangelists and I was bothered by how these preachers were like beggars—always asking for more money! It seemed like most of a preacher's job was involved in raising funds for the church, missions, and ministries instead of actually helping people. The Bible says, 'freely you have received, freely give.' How can you charge people for the good news of the Gospel?

I knew I wanted to preach—I had been preaching for a while already—but I didn't want to be a preacher like that: I didn't want to depend on men for money. If people paid me to preach, then I would be obligated to please them, to speak what they wanted to hear. If I want people to pay me more, than they have to like me and like what I am saying, but I didn't want that. I wanted to be a free agent, out to please God not man.

God, I was talking to God while watching people walk by, all the riches of the Earth are yours already. I imagined all the money these people walking by had. Everything they had, came from God already. Everything I made was his first. Lord, I want to do your will. You own everything! Why don't you give me enough to do your work? Bless me, Lord, so I don't have to beg. Why should I need to rely on man when I have a Father who wants to give me good things? My mind went back to the Televangelists on TV, how they would do and say anything just to get people to send them money. Where was God in that? Give me enough to go and do your work, I prayed.

I stood up from the curb and went to find some Pepsi. God had been so good to me. He had never let me down. I knew with a certainty that he would be my provider. I might not have much now, but I could already see far off that I would always have more than enough. I might even be rich one day—and it wouldn't be from asking people for money—it would be from God: his blessings in my life, his hand guiding my steps, and his wisdom in my actions.

I worshipped him the rest of the day, thanking him for what he was doing in my life, and for what I already knew he was going to do in my future.

CHAPTER TWENTY-FOUR

# OFFENDED

A traveling Evangelist, Bud, was in town doing a tent meeting and boy did I admire him! He had a heart after God like I couldn't believe—he'd cry when he talked about what God meant to him—and he always had time to mingle with the people of the church after the meetings. I wanted to get to know him, to rub shoulders with him and learn his ways. Maybe some of his anointing would be passed on to me if I could spend some time with him.

After one such meeting I finally got my chance to talk to him.

"Great message tonight," I began, approaching him to shake his hand.

"Thanks, son," he said smiling. "Say, would you like to go for coffee when we clear out here?"

"Sure," I said.

"You got a car?"

"Yeah, you want a ride?"

"That'd be good. I've got two people that need a ride along too. You have room?"

"Whatever you want, I can do it."

"Good, I'll see you in say half an hour," he slapped my shoulder and turned to the person beside me to talk.

I walked away excited and went to get my car ready.

In a half hour the minister walked out of the church with his arm around a young girl. A boy was trailing along behind and both kids were the children of prominent members of our church. I knew them fairly well and I was surprised their parents were letting them come along at this hour. But what did I know? I was sure it was fine.

He climbed into the back seat with the girl and the boy sat up front with me.

I pulled out of the parking lot and began making my way to the restaurant we were going to. "I really liked what you said tonight," I said, keeping my eyes on the road ahead, "how you explained the...."

Bud wasn't answering me. I glanced into the rearview mirror, but it was too dark in the back seat to see anything. I turned around to make sure he heard me. When I turned I couldn't believe what I saw. Bud had one hand in the girl's hair and one on her leg and was kissing her. I quickly turned back to the front. I felt sick. My pulse was racing. I could hardly believe what I had seen. There was no way I was mistaken though. I stayed silent the rest of the ride until we pulled into the restaurant.

There was a group of young people waiting there when we arrived. Bud had invited quite a group of people. I was disappointed this wouldn't be the one-on-one time I had anticipated, and at the same time I was relieved, because I was still trying to wrap my mind around what had just happened.

We found a table and Bud sat directly between two young girls. He was smiling and teasing them, his hands under the table. I couldn't believe how blatant he was being about it all. Then he started making inappropriate jokes and I couldn't take it anymore. I stood up. "You have betrayed my trust." I pointed my finger at him and walked out, not bothering to wait for a reply.

I walked out of the restaurant feeling completely broken hearted. What a creep! How could he talk like he knew God and loved him and yet he was playing around with young girls while he was married? And these girls were young! They didn't know any better!

I felt embarrassed for ever wanting to be with a guy like that.

When I got home Lorraine was waiting for me. "How did it go?" She asked.

I couldn't even answer her. I just stared at her for a moment and shook my head. I went into the bedroom and fell onto the bed exhausted. I felt so offended. I was so innocent in God—I was just a babe in the Lord then—and this man had hurt me and used me.

Why had he asked me for coffee at all? Had he just used me for a ride? Or had he thought I might join in on his actions? Was this what ministers were doing? I felt sick thinking how he had put on an act during his services and then snuck around like a snake afterwards, defiling young people.

Why was it no matter where I looked I was always let down by my leaders? Was there no one truly who could teach me the ways of God? How would I ever learn without a teacher I could trust?

For over a year I didn't tell anyone what I had seen. But when I met Bud in a chance encounter, I confronted him. "You have offended me," I said, not giving him a chance to answer, "And whosoever shall offend one of these little ones that believe in me, it is better for him that a millstone were hanged about his neck, and he was cast into the sea." I turned and walked away. How many lives he ruined I don't know—maybe I should have done more than just confront him—maybe I should have reported him, but I knew eventually his deeds would catch up with him. And I wasn't wrong.

CHAPTER TWENTY-FIVE

# THE PROPHECY

I was driving home from work one day, taking a different route than usual when the Word of the Lord came to me, "Go to Waves of Glory Church and I will speak to you there."

I pulled up in front of the building Sunday evening. Most people were inside already. I pushed through the doors and quickly found a seat right behind a guy twice my size, so the speaker wouldn't be able to make eye contact with me.

The service started as I sat there waiting. I didn't know what to expect except that God had said he would speak to me and I knew he would.

"There's somebody in here that God wants to speak to." My mind snapped to attention, but I didn't move. I could almost feel the pastor searching the crowd for me.

"I can't see you," the pastor said, "but God wants to speak to you." He was quiet a moment, searching. Finally he pointed to the centre.

"Me?" A lady three rows up asks.

"No, behind you."

He was still looking. I felt already he knew just where I was.

"Me?" Two rows up.

"No. Behind you,"

"Is it me?" The man in front of me asked.

"I can't see him, but he's behind you." He must have caught a glimpse of my shirt sleeve.

"You!" He said, "In the white shirt behind that man. Come out. God has something to say to you."

Finally, I moved over to catch a glimpse of the pastor. "Me?" I asked.

"Yes, come to the front." I made my way to the aisle and down to the front. "Let's bow our heads," he said to the congregation. Then he came down and stood beside me.

He looked right into my eyes and placed his hand on my shoulder, "Can I pray for you?"

"Okay." I said.

He closed his eyes and said a prayer. I couldn't even really hear it because my heart was pounding so hard. The pastor opened his eyes and said quietly, "The Lord wants to say to you:

> "Surely I have called you, my son. Stop speaking out of your own head. Stop speaking out of your own heart. Learn to move when my spirit moves. When I put my words in your mouth and I tell you to speak, that's when you speak. Then men will say, 'what great things He has done for you'... and you will preach both in this age and the age to come."

The words sunk deep into my soul and engraved themselves in my mind. I knew I had been preaching from my head. Messages from other people that I had memorized so that people would think I was a good preacher. Without those messages I didn't have anything to say! I wouldn't be a good preacher anymore.

I felt my pride rise up within me, but at the same time I felt the stronger presence of my inner man. I wanted to do what was right. I wanted to preach what God gave me to say, not what other people had to say. I had been preaching vain words with no power. Give me words to say, Lord, and I will say them, I prayed. And when you're not in it—I won't speak!

That vow resonated into the deepest part of me. From now on I would only preach what God wanted me to—his words, and his power.

CHAPTER TWENTY-SIX

# THE FIRST CLEAR MESSAGE

It still bothered me that I couldn't speak in tongues. Every service I would sit and talk to God, and ask why he wasn't letting me speak in tongues like everyone else. I knew I couldn't get the Holy Spirit unless I spoke in tongues. John had told me tongues was the sign that you had the Spirit of God in you. I was preaching and ministering in the church, but I couldn't manifest the Holy Spirit. What was wrong with me?

Yet God was working in me, showing me things.

One Sunday morning I was sitting in my pew watching the service. I felt myself look up at someone across the room. It was my inner man showing me someone and I knew God had something to say to him.

I went over to him and spoke, "Once you walked with God, but you're not there anymore. You parked your wagon and you're not serving God anymore. But I've got something to tell you. God is drawing you. Come back tonight and God will set you free. You will have what you want. You will get back what you lost, and much more." The man looked at me with tears in his eyes. I had told him exactly what he was feeling, what had been happening to him.

But I wasn't amazed at what I had said, God had said it through me. I didn't know anything about that man but God knew him.

I went back to my church pew and sat down. I was struggling now.

*"Lord, are you going to give that man your Holy Spirit, and keep it from me?"* I was crying inside. God had promised his Spirit to his people, yet he hadn't given it to me. Why not? *Lord,* I thought, *you better not do it.* I felt angry. *I've been asking you for that for years. I don't get it and everybody else gets it?*

That night at the service there was an altar call, and, sure enough, the man I had talked to went up. I stood behind him a bit, watching. People thought I was praying, but I wasn't. I was watching his every move. When he began to speak in tongues I turned and walked away. *Lord, why do you use me to say things to people, but when it comes to me, I never get it?* I pushed through the doors of the church into the cool night air. *What was wrong with me? Was I not good enough?* I felt so confused. I took a deep breath. I wanted this more than anything. I turned back into the building and walked straight to the front.

"Pray for me!" I said to John as I lifted my hands to God and waited.

John met me at the altar with a vial of oil. "People of God!" he announced, turning to the congregation. "Pray now together in unity for Brother Art!"

I felt hands being placed on me. I felt oil smeared on my forehead and a hot hand pressing against my head almost putting me off balance. But I didn't care. I stood, waiting for God to give me his Spirit. Pastor John began to pray louder, his hand shaking on my head. I felt oil drip down my hair onto my face and neck. People all around were shouting and speaking in tongues. Hands rubbed the oil over me, over my back and sides. I smelled the thick scent of myrrh the oil held. I was crying.

"Speak!" I heard someone say. "Let the words come out!" Someone grabbed me by the jaw and tried to open and shut my mouth.

I wasn't going to fake the Spirit. I wasn't going to let my mouth speak words I was making up. I cried harder to God. *Lord, do your will in me!* Hands all around were shaking me, pushing me. Women were rubbing their hands up and down my sides, and it was making me uncomfortable! They were shouting and crying so loudly I couldn't concentrate anymore. If God was going to do anything for me it was fading fast. I felt my arms drop beside me. I pushed the hands away from me and fell to my knees, weeping.

It was over. God was not going to put his Spirit in me.

"Do not lose faith," John said to me, his hand on my back. "The church will fast for you. You must fast too. Something in your life is blocking God from working in you. Fast, and next week we will go to a revival in North Dakota. The Spirit has been falling on the people there."

John announced loudly to the church, "I am asking you all to fast this week for Brother Art. Next Sunday God will move mightily in him."

I stayed there on my knees at the altar long after the service ended. I felt God settle over me like a cloak, that familiar presence that I had grown to recognize as my father, my protector, my comforter. He was so good to me, I truly felt like I was his son, and even though I was hurt he watched over me and filled me with peace.

CHAPTER TWENTY-SEVEN

# PURPLE GAS

A week later we packed the kids into our car and headed to Golden Valley North Dakota in a caravan with the rest of the church. It was an exciting time, traveling into the US. The kids were rolling around in the back seat shouting excitedly at every new thing they saw. Lorraine and I sat in the front. She wasn't talking much but I was fine with that because my mind was focused on what was going to happen this weekend. I was going to get the Spirit of God even if it killed me.

When we stopped at a gas station to fill up, I didn't pull up to the pump like the other people. I parked my car, opened the trunk and pulled out two cans of gas I had brought along. It was a cheaper, dyed gas used by farmers and I liked to keep a few jugs on hand when I could.

When we got to Golden Valley there was already a meeting going on. The parking lot was packed with cars and vans, people coming from all over to be in the presence of these speakers. Rumours had spread like wildfire that the Spirit of God was falling heavily in this place. Even from out in the parking you could hear the pastor shouting, the music playing, and the shouts and cries of the people.

The speaker that night was a fiery one. He jumped around the stage, spit when he yelled, and liked to shout out an "oh hallelujah" every couple of seconds followed by a few words in tongues. "When the day of Pentecost had come, hallelujah, they were all together in one place!" He spread his arm about the assembly, his face was red and sweaty from shouting, his voice hoarse, "And suddenly a sound came from heaven like the rush of a mighty wind! Hallelujah!" He went off into tongues, "And it filled all the house where they were sitting! Is the Spirit here, people of God? Are you filled?" He yelled. "Hallelujah! And there appeared to them tongues as of fire, distributed and resting on each one of them." He wiped his brow. "The Holy Ghost is a fire! Is there a fire burning on you today? Can you feel the fire of God in you? Oh Hallelujah!" He went off into more tongues. "And they were all filled with the Holy Spirit and began to speak in tongues!"

Here he stopped and lifted his hands over the assembly. "Tonight all will be filled with the Holy Ghost! Let's praise him!" Music swayed in and around the assembly, filling the room, moving the people with the emotion of the words and the music. Many were crying and calling out to God.

"God has promised the people of God his Spirit," the pastor said, more quietly now. "Are you going to receive that spirit today?" He scanned the crowd with his eyes. "Come forward now, come stand in the presence of God. I'm going to pray for you. There are people here who need the Spirit of God."

I didn't even bother to hesitate. This is what I was here for. I walked down the aisle, John close behind me, ready to pray with the pastor for me. I wasn't alone though. Hundreds of people were flooding the aisles and heading down to the altar.

If I thought the other times I had been prayed for with oil were bad—this was the hardest most valiant effort I had ever endured. When my turn came to be prayed for, John spoke quietly to the minister, probably explaining my situation. I felt the pastor come up beside me, speaking in tongues, breathing heavily and whispering 'oh hallelujah' every couple of seconds. He held a vial of oil in his hands and his hands were wet and glistening from the others he had already prayed for. Most people he had approached had just instantly fallen over and started shaking on the floor and speaking in tongues.

I stood, as I always had, wanting a real experience with the Spirit of God.

The prayers began, John on one side and this pastor on the other. "The promise has gone out, Brother Art. The spirit of God will fall on you today! You must embrace it! Let the Holy Ghost speak through you! Don't be afraid to utter the words of the spirit!"

He touched my head with oil and shouted suddenly, *"TONGUES OF FIRE, FALL!"*

That had worked for the others, but I didn't feel anything. He prayed some more, calling on God.

"Brother Art, is there some sin in your life you are hiding from God?"

I thought about it. I had a lot of sin but I never hid any of it. My sins were forgiven weren't they? "I don't think so," I said.

Nothing happened. I stood there until the end of service, but never once did I feel the Spirit of God.

After the service I was heading out to the car with Lorraine and the kids when John approached me.

"Art, what kind of gas have you got in your car?"

I looked at him in disbelief. "What does purple gas have to do with God giving me the Holy Spirit?"

John heard the ridiculousness of it but he needed to save face. There must be some reason I wasn't speaking in tongues and it couldn't have anything to do with him or this meeting.

"You know what," I said, "I'm starting to think that what you have—I don't want it." I turned and walked away.

"Art, wait!" John called after me but I didn't turn.

I didn't speak in tongues, but the more I thought about it, I saw the power of God in my life. They had tongues, but I didn't see any power in them! We drove home that night and the whole time I couldn't help but be disappointed in what had happened at the meeting. What a poor excuse it was that a pastor had to blame the gas I used as a reason for me not speaking in tongues. Why did the church believe you had to be perfect for God to give something to you?

I thought about that time God first spoke to me in the mud. I didn't deserve anything from God, but I sure needed him. If I were perfect, I wouldn't need God in my life. Maybe that was the catch. It was my brokenness and my faults that kept me dependant on God. I knew that it was Him in me that did the miracles, not anything I did in the flesh. If God wasn't giving me His Spirit it wasn't because I used purple gas, I knew that for sure. I would just have to keep waiting.

CHAPTER TWENTY-EIGHT

# THE SPIRIT OF GOD

For four more years I struggled to understand why, no matter how hard I tried, I couldn't speak in tongues. It was such a difficult time for me. I was speaking in the churches, traveling around as a minister, evangelizing, praying, preaching, prophesying—but I never uttered a word in tongues. I felt hurt. I just couldn't understand why my Father would keep his Spirit from me.

It was finally in the spring of 1978 at a revival meeting in Saskatoon that God touched me. I was kneeling at the altar, like I always did, calling out to God, when my friend came up beside me. He was quiet, but I could feel him beside me. Maybe he was praying for me, I'm not sure, but I'll never forget how he stopped me. He put a hand on my face and turned me to face him.

"Art—"

I met his calm and confident eyes—while my own were hurt and searching. "What?"

"You have the Spirit of God."

I can't explain that feeling that comes over you when you finally believe something. It's like a light comes on, and suddenly you can see everything and you wonder how you never saw it that way before. For me, my mind lit up. I saw everything clearly for the first time and I knew it was true. I did have the Spirit of God, I'd had it all along! I just hadn't believed it. My mind had been dark. God said when we receive his spirit we would receive power and I felt that power in me now, like a live current ready to illuminate anything I touched.

I jumped up right there and began to praise God. I saw what he'd done for me. I saw the miracles he had performed through me, the things he had shown me. How could those things have been done without the Spirit of God working in me and through me?

I mounted the stage that evening, stood behind the pulpit and preached the best sermon I'd ever preached. Not a word of it had been prepared. I don't remember the words I spoke that night, but I remember the results. People were touched, lives were changed, many people repented and were converted. I even remember John standing up in the crowd and watching me with wonder. He saw the change in me as clearly as if I had been just a drawing of myself before and now I had suddenly come to life! I had the Spirit of God in me. I had the power of God working through me and he couldn't deny that. Whether I spoke in tongues or not, I had the Spirit of God: I believed now—and I would forevermore be changed.

The church might give you a license to preach, but it's God that gives you power. The church wants you to preach what they want you to preach, and if they like you they give you a license and call you a minister. But when God gave me his Holy Spirit, that same day he gave me power so I can do his service.

CHAPTER TWENTY-NINE

# GOD HEALS!

Two of my brothers came to the Lord around the same time I did, and God had done amazing things in both of their lives. Who would have thought three of Joe Adam's kids would become preachers?

I always attested it to my mother's prayers. She always said she asked God to bless her by making one of her sons a priest…well, she never got that, but he gave her three preachers instead!

I was invited by my brothers to a meeting in Ontario. They wanted me to preach there. It was a house meeting and while I was preaching I spoke by the Spirit and power of God. Later when the service was over I heard them talking together, "I can't get over what God has done for him." They had known me all my life and, seeing me now, they couldn't believe the change. They didn't know I could hear them, but their words confirmed the prophecy I had received at Waves of Glory just a year before: men will say, 'what great things God has done for you.'

One day I was speaking at a service in Treherne when my eyes fastened on a boy there. He looked to be about fourteen and I knew right away God wanted to do something for him. I went up to him after the service. "Hey," I said, "God told me he wants to do something for you. Can I pray for you?"

The boy looked up at me and there was hope deep in his eyes.

"Yes," he said.

I laid my hands on the boy. God had shown me people to pray for before and he had always done what he said he would do. This would be no different. "Lord, you showed me this boy when I was speaking, and you want to heal him. Father, you are so good! And it is nothing for you to heal his back. You want to do it! Restore his back to health in Jesus' name!" I lifted my hands and looked at the boy.

He was crying, both his hands covering his face. He wiped his eyes and reached behind his back to feel his spine. It had straightened up! I heard the snaps as he undid the brace he had on and slid it out from behind him. "I'm healed," he said in shock. He felt his back again and turned from side to side. Then he looked back at me—his face lit up with a grin. "I can't believe it! My back is totally fine! Thank you!" He dropped the brace on the floor beside him.

That boy might have been excited about what God had done but I felt even more excited! Every day that passed, every miracle I witnessed, every time I felt God move in me, my faith grew. This is how you receive faith! By God working through you. By God moving in your life. Our faith is ever-increasing. Every time God does a miracle it increases your faith.

CHAPTER THIRTY

## A VOICE THROUGH THE CROWD

I was speaking at a meeting in Winnipeg one evening with two of my friends from church. After the service I was talking with a group of people. It was so loud in the room you could barely hear your own words coming out of your mouth. There were so many people. All of a sudden I heard a voice say, "Romack." It was so clear. I stopped talking and turned to look through the crowd of over two hundred people. There, at the back of the room my eyes fastened on a man and I knew that was the man who had said the name "Romack." God had carried that voice straight to my ear. There's no way I could have heard that otherwise.

"Follow me," I said to my two friends, "watch what God's going to do." I made my way quickly through the crowd.

"Excuse me," I said, coming up beside the man. He looked at me, slightly shocked.

"Yes?"

"I couldn't help but hear. Did you say Romack?" The man must have thought I had been standing nearby the whole time, because there's no way I could have heard that from where I had been standing.

"Yeah. He's been admitted to the hospital. They say he doesn't have much time."

"Which hospital?"

"St. Boniface. Do you know him?"

I didn't answer. I turned to my friends who had followed me. "Come on," I said, hurrying through the crowd. "God is going to heal this man."

When God shows me something, I receive a faith that is not of myself. I don't think it's going to happen. I know it is.

We got into the car and headed to the hospital. When we got to Romack's room I suddenly felt unsure about what I was supposed to do or say. I knocked on the door and peered into the room.

A man was lying on the bed with his eyes closed but he awoke at the knock.

"Can we come in?" I asked.

He nodded weakly.

"I'm here to pray for you," I said. "God showed me he was going to heal you."

Romack grimaced, he looked like he was in pain. "Go ahead."

I went up to his bedside and my two friends followed. I could see in my mind already what to do, "God you showed me that you want to heal this man. I ask, Lord, that you would heal his body from his head to his toes." I placed my hand on his head. "Sickness, leave this man's body in Jesus' name."

That's it. The man opened his eyes. He didn't look any different and maybe he didn't feel any different. I don't know. There was no evidence that anything had happened, but I knew that something had. I had been obedient to what God had asked me to do and I had total faith that God would do what he said.

I was at work the next day, getting into my truck for lunch, when I heard God say to me, "Romack has been healed." The words were as clear as the first time God spoke to me. I knew the work had been done. I looked down at my watch—it was twelve o clock noon.

I went back to the hospital that evening to talk to Romack. I wanted to see if he had been healed. He was sitting up in his bed when I entered and his face brightened when he saw me.

"Art! You'll never guess what happened," he said. "I had cancer and the doctors said I didn't have much time left to live but today at noon God healed me!"

"I knew it!" I said. I was excited! "Today at work God spoke to me and told me you were healed and it was right at twelve o clock!"

"Thank you," the man said to me, "and praise God!"

I walked out of the room encouraged. It must be an incredible feeling to be healed by the hand of God—but it's just as incredible to be the one God uses to heal. I felt elated—so full of joy and excitement for what God had done. He uses ordinary people to do his supernatural work. We just have to be obedient to his voice. I wanted God in my life and now here he was working in me and through me for his good pleasure. Seeing this miracle only made me love God more, and more determined to serve him no matter what would come against me.

## CHAPTER THIRTY-ONE

## GOD SPEAKS TO HIS CHILDREN

John was in Cleveland one week for the general assembly and I was taking over preaching at our church that Sunday. It was the evening service and I was speaking a message called 'pressing towards the mark' and I felt the Lord.

God had given me the spirit of discernment, and as I looked through the crowd I saw a boy. Somehow I knew he was sick. I called the boy to the front and said, "You're sick."

"I'm really sick," he said to me.

The presence of the Lord was there to heal. "Can I pray for you?" I asked. "God wants to heal you."

I took the vial of oil that was always present at the pulpit, tipped some onto my finger and touched him on the forehead. There was no great act, no great words, just a simple prayer to my Father asking him to heal this boy, but as I prayed I felt the Lord right there with me and I knew the healing would be done.

It wasn't until after the service later that night that I got a call from John's wife, Ruth, in Cleveland.

"Brother Art, you won't believe what happened," she began.

"Try me."

"We were at the assembly for the evening service, when right at eight o'clock a lady in the pew in front of us turned around and said to me, 'Your son has been healed.'"

"That was right when I had prayed for him!" I said excitedly.

"Well, we got home after the service and called up our son. We asked him how the service had gone at church. He said you prayed for him and he had been healed! Just like the lady said."

"Wow! Praise God."

"What a miracle!" Ruth said. "Brother Art, I've never seen the Lord work through anyone like he works through you."

I didn't know what to say. "You know it's got nothing to do with me," I said. "God asks me to pray, I pray—that's the only way I can describe it."

"Well, thank you," Ruth said. "And I will see you when we get home ! Have a good night."

"You too." Ruth hung up and I marvelled at the work God had done tonight. How hundreds of miles away he would let Ruth know that her son was healed. To me that was just as much a miracle as the healing itself: that God speaks to his children, that he uses man to do his work. How blessed are we! People marvelled at the work Jesus was doing among the people and he said to them 'Greater works will you do because I go to my Father.'

## CHAPTER THIRTY-TWO

# THE TABERNACLE

"Art, I'd like you to go to Cleveland for the pastoral training program. You're preaching a lot now and it's time you got your minister's license with the church," John said to me one day.

I knew it meant taking two weeks off of work, which is why I had been delaying going for so long—but it was true, I had been wanting to get my ministers license, and this was as good a time as any.

"Alright John, I'll go," I said, "but when I get back don't expect me to only preach at this church. I will still go around to other churches."

John looked irritated. He didn't like it when I went to other churches as he was always afraid of losing me. When I spoke, I usually brought a crowd. I had stuck with the church, even though I knew now I didn't have to speak in tongues to have the Spirit, but I remained leery now of the church doctrines. I knew that man could be misled, and I no longer put my trust in what the church leaders had to say. That made me a bit of a threat, but it also made me more of an attraction. People were drawn to the passion and charisma I displayed, and even though they didn't always like what I had to say, there was no denying the power of God that moved through me.

"You do what you need to do," John said, nodding.

Cleveland was great. I went with my two friends from church, Jerry and Dave. We met so many people at the training program, everyone with a heart to minister and spread the word of God. I found myself wishing I had gone sooner. Every day we spent hours in a classroom at the head Church of God of Prophecy. There were hundreds of young men and women eager to learn and preach. Many of the men and women were there as couples, and I would watch them stroll across the lawn holding hands. Just seeming so happy to serve the Lord together, I felt sad. I wanted to be able to have my wife by my side in the ministry too. I wanted to be able to share these experiences with her! But Lorraine, although she was a part of the church now, did not like to work with me.

Things were busy and we were studying and learning all day and long into the evenings. When we went to bed at night we were exhausted.

One night in the middle of a deep sleep, I suddenly woke up and heard God saying, *'Someone will ask you to speak at the Tabernacle.'* I was so tired, I wasn't sure what had happened. I looked over at the clock on the nightstand and the red numbers shone two o'clock. I fell back onto my pillow and instantly dropped back into a deep sleep. Exactly one hour later I sat up again and heard the same thing: *'Someone is going to ask you to speak at the Tabernacle.'* This time I reached for my notebook and a pencil. I wrote down the message, pulled the sheet of paper out of my book and stuck it into the bedside drawer. Then I was able to drop back to sleep and slept the rest of the night.

The next morning when I got up I told my roommates, Jerry and Dave, "God spoke to me."

"What did you hear?" they asked.

"I'm not telling you, but I wrote it down. It's in the dorm rooms."

I saw them exchange glances, doubting me, maybe, but it didn't matter. They had been with me long enough to know that God did strange things through me. "When it happens," I said, "I'll show you the paper as proof."

Sure enough, during the last break of the day everyone was milling about in the classroom, talking, eating, enjoying the time to move around instead of being stuck in the desks. My attention was caught by someone moving through the crowd, looking around. I knew right away they were looking for me. I grabbed Jerry by the shoulder, "Jerry! Dave! Watch this. There's someone coming, and they're going to ask me something—and it's the same thing I wrote down in the dorm room."

Jerry looked incredulous.

The man came through the crowd and finally arrived at my desk.

"What's your name?" he asked.

"Adam," I replied.

"Arthur Adam?"

"Yes."

"How would you like to preach at the Tabernacle this Wednesday?"

"Why sure!" I could hardly contain my excitement. I wasn't excited so much that they had chosen me, I knew it was nothing I had done that made them choose me but I was excited because God had shown me in advance! When you think about a God like that, and how he makes himself real to you, it's humbling, but it's exciting too!

My roommates could hardly believe it when I showed them the note I had scribbled in my notebook the night before. "God really speaks to you," they said. "I wish he spoke to me that way."

I called my parents up that night to tell them the news.

"I hope you don't make a fool of yourself," was all my mom had to say. Well, what had I expected? Lorraine didn't sound very excited either, but John sure was.

"I'll make sure to tune into the radio to hear you!" he said. "This is great news, Art! Good for you!"

As I stood that Wednesday evening looking in the mirror I felt proud. I couldn't help but think back fifteen years ago to the first time I'd looked in a mirror and seen myself. I had been only fifteen years old, kicked out of home with nothing. I had believed I was ugly and stupid and, when I had looked in the mirror, I had seen nothing but a reject. I had felt so dirty and unwanted. *How can anyone stand to even look at me?* I had thought.

Now I was a completely different person. I was strong and handsome. I had money and success. I had confidence. And most of all I had found a family that accepted me and was proud of me and had chosen me to be a leader among them!

I wished I could have gone back in time to tell that young boy things would get better! I wouldn't always be the 'Adams boy from St. Labre.' Look what God was doing in me. Look what he had made of me. I was nothing, but he was everything. I felt like I had hit the jackpot. God had transformed my life, I wasn't the same man I had been a few years before, lost, desperate, alone and without hope. God was real, and he had made his presence known in my life and I loved him for it! He wasn't using me because I was good—I knew I wasn't. The Lord did things in *spite* of me, because I loved him.

"You ready?" my roommate stuck his head in the bathroom door. "We've got to go or we'll be late!"

"Coming!" I straightened my satin striped tie, smoothed my hair, grabbed my suit jacket and headed out the door. "Let's go!"

The Tabernacle held ten thousand people. It was a big crowd when I went up to speak. I felt honoured to be able to preach to these people.

"If my people who are called by my name," I said as I felt a passion burning in me, "would humble themselves and pray…." My words echoed through the auditorium. These people were watching my every move. I couldn't get over the fact that God had chosen me to speak. These people would never have chosen me if they knew me at all—but somehow I had been chosen. I preached the message and came off the stage. Jerry and Dave were there to meet me when I finished.

"I was blessed by that message," Jerry said.

"I'm glad they picked you," Dave said. "I wouldn't have been able to do that."

I knew it wasn't me. If it had been my message, I would have been nervous and messed everything up, but ever since God had given me his power to preach, the messages just flowed out of me. I felt elated!

After preaching that message everyone seemed to recognize me! It was so strange, walking down the street in Cleveland and people would come up to me and greet me and say, " I heard you preach at the Tabernacle!"

I would just shy away. "I'm glad you enjoyed it," I would say.

Some people asked me later in life "Don't you have pride? Didn't you ever feel lifted up by the things God used you for?" I can honestly say I never did. I *knew* where I came from. I *knew* that nothing about that message or even the opportunity to speak it was of me.

## CHAPTER THIRTY-THREE

# HEALING LAURA'S LEG

It was a beautiful summer evening and I was at home with Lorraine and the kids. We were all out playing on the lawn and I was taking the kids for rides on the handlebars of our bike. I had my youngest, Laura, up on the handlebars now and she was squealing and laughing with delight as I wheeled down the driveway.

"Faster Papa!" she cried, her blonde curls blowing in the breeze.

I pedalled faster, holding her around the waist securely with one hand and steering with the other. Everything happened so fast. I felt her slip and try to catch herself. She stuck her foot down over the wheel and suddenly she screamed and we were both falling. I had a sick feeling in my stomach because I had felt the bike lurch and I knew her leg must have gotten stuck in the wheel spokes.

I must have been in shock as I stood over her. Everything else around me was gone, just my daughter lying on the ground, and her leg bent oddly and mangled. I didn't think, I just felt my soul cry out. I reached out my hand over her leg, "Lord, heal her." I couldn't bare to see my daughter in pain from something I had done. I straightened her leg, my soul crying out to God the whole time.

Lorraine ran over to us, "What happened?" she cried.

"Her leg," I said, but I couldn't explain more. "Get the car, Lorraine."

I scooped Laura up in my arms. She was crying and holding onto me tightly. "It's going to be ok," I assured her. "We are going to make sure you're ok."

I drove her to the hospital emergency, but by the time we got there she had stopped crying and was sniffling quietly in the back seat. I lifted her out and carried her into the hospital. Her leg was red and maybe a bruise was forming, but it looked perfectly straight.

The doctors took an x-ray to be safe and they were surprised I had brought her in. "Just a bruise," they said. "Her leg looks fine."

I knew better. Her leg had been totally bent and broken, but God had healed her. I hugged her close as we left the hospital.

"My leg doesn't hurt anymore, Papa," she said, leaning her head on my shoulder, "It was broken in the bike, but it's not anymore."

"I know Laura. God healed you."

"Yep!" She smiled at me, "Can I ride on the handlebars again when we get home?"

I laughed. "No Laura, Papa has learned his lesson. No more handlebar rides!"

"Awe," she frowned, but then brightened slightly. "Well, when I'm older I will ride the bike by myself," she looked at me proudly. "And then I can give *you* a ride. Right Papa?"

I laughed as we headed home to give Lorraine the news. Laura was fine!

CHAPTER THIRTY-FOUR

# SEEING THE SPIRIT MAN

I was preaching every chance I got now. A couple church friends and I would travel around as guest speakers to any church and town that would take us. Revival meetings and tent meetings were a big movement at that time and it wasn't too hard to find a place where we could talk. I talked to anyone as I was always looking for someone to talk to about God.

God was constantly showing me spiritual things. I would look at a person and see things about their life that other people couldn't see! Especially spiritual things.

Once in church I noticed a man sitting not far away. I could see he was bound—no one else could see it—but there was a snake wrapped around him, keeping him in bondage. It was a spirit and he needed to be set free. People were always shocked when I talked about spirits in church. Most people thought spirits were only in bad people, like drug addicts or people who did witchcraft. People have asked me 'How can a Christian have spirits?' I always said, "Why would Jesus go to church to cast out Devils if Christians (people in Church) don't have spirits?" Religious people could have spirits as easily as anyone else and I could see it all around me. I'm not saying there's a devil behind every bush but this stuff exists. People wonder how you can have God in you and a devil in you at the same time. Spirits inhabit the flesh. God dwells in the inner man!

I was beginning to understand that the spirit in me, the inner man, had eyes. My inner man could see things that my flesh could not. God would show me things, teaching me about the inner man.

I was driving home one day on Nairn Avenue when I saw an accident up ahead. It was dark out and I could see the flashing lights of the emergency response vehicles and the orange glow of the fire. I felt an urgency to see what was going on. I drove as close as I could get, then pulled over and jumped out of my truck.

I jogged along the ditch and came up opposite the truck. I was close enough to see everything. The truck had flipped over and burst into flames. The fire truck was putting out the flames while the ambulance attendants waited to get close enough to start rescuing the victims. I could just make out a pair of arms draped over the steering wheel and another person in the passenger seat.

As I watched the two men being burned in the truck, I looked over and suddenly they were standing beside me. They were standing there, watching their bodies burn. How could I see that? I didn't know. Two men died that night in the accident. It was confirmed in a news report later.

CHAPTER THIRTY-FIVE

# CALLED TO BE A PROPHET

The sky was an eerie yellow. My brother and I were working a job putting pipes underground near Ste. Anne when the wind began to pick up. I didn't think much of it as the weather didn't usually stop us from working. I was in my machine, digging up the ground to gain access to the underground pipes when I felt the hairs on my arms and the back of my neck stand on end. I looked up and saw a funnel of black was twisting out of the sky, thick and ferocious, making a path straight towards us.

"Look!" I called to my brother across the yard. "There's a tornado coming!"

I jumped out of the backhoe and was hit with a blast of wind and dirt. The wind nearly ripped the door off the hinges behind me as it banged and rattled against the machine. It sounded like a freight train was heading straight for us. My brother was running towards me, his eyes terrified.

"Get in the truck!" I yelled. I grabbed my brother by the collar and dragged him with me towards the truck.

"Where are we going to go?" he asked as I fumbled with the keys trying to jam them into the ignition. The truck started with a loud rumble, but I couldn't even hear it over the thunder of the tornado heading our way.

"Anywhere where that thing isn't going!" I slammed the truck into gear and tore out of the yard. We sped down the highway and pulled into a small restaurant just off the road. There wasn't time to get any farther.

We burst through the doors of the restaurant, taking cover from the wind and the rain that was now pelting. Everyone in the restaurant was gathered at the windows, staring in shock.

"We need to take cover!" My brother said, pulling me away from the windows. But I couldn't move. I stood watching the frothing whirlwind make its way towards us. Debris flying everywhere, boards and branches started to hit the windows of the restaurant.

"Look," someone said, pointing out the window. We all watched in horror as a tractor got lifted up by the tornado and spun around like it weighed no more than a child's toy. The funnel tore through a building, sending roofing and concrete flying. That's when we all took action.

"Get down!" someone shouted.

"Away from the windows!" Another person warned. My brother and I dragged a table towards the back wall that thankfully had no windows, and we were quickly joined by the other diners, dragging tables and chairs, tipping them over so we could all huddle under them and pray the tornado passed us by unharmed.

The roar of the wind outside was thunderous. I can't compare it to anything I've heard before. Pure power. The ground shook, dishes rattled, the hanging lights swung above our heads casting shadows. The power flickered and then went out, but I barely noticed with so much commotion going on outside the restaurant. We couldn't see anything out the windows now, except debris whipping around.

Then, as quickly as it had started, it calmed. The rattling stopped, the thundering abated, everything became still. Slowly we climbed out from underneath the table. Still no one had spoken. I walked to the restaurant door and opened it to step outside.

There was carnage everywhere. It looked like a bomb had been dropped. My brother came up behind me and walked over to our truck. It was wet and covered with leaves and dirt from the wind, but otherwise unscathed.

I got in beside him and we drove off to get a look at the damage. All along the highway telephone poles had been ripped out of the ground and tossed across the fields. Strips of asphalt had been torn out of the highway. There was debris everywhere. I could see a car flipped over in a field—who knows how far it had been carried in the wind.

"How did we survive that?" I asked my brother, who looked as shocked as I felt.

"That tornado turned right at the restaurant." My brother confirmed what I had been thinking, "We were right in its path and it turned."

The evidence was all around us.

I had never seen such power as I had seen in that storm. The fury of the wind, the strength of that funnel cloud—how it had ripped up asphalt, flipped boxcars, lifted tractors—yet that power had been redirected as easily as if it were an animal obeying its master. God had stopped that tornado from hitting us. I knew it as surely as I knew we would have died had God not intervened.

We couldn't finish our job with the pipes because the devastation from the storm had damaged too much to continue. We cleaned up what we could and left our separate ways.

As I drove home the radio was already reporting on the storm. Two men had taken shelter in a train boxcar and had died when the tornado had flipped that boxcar like it was made of straw.

Why had God intervened to save me? I didn't deserve his protection, I wasn't any different than any other person, probably even worse than most people. I had a temper and I was headstrong, stubborn. I had gotten my girlfriend pregnant out of wedlock. Even now we didn't really get along and I often found myself wishing I were with someone else. Why did God bother with me? I wasn't good by any means.

But I loved God. And this made me love him even more. I couldn't understand why he had decided to look down on me and help—but he had—and I was forever grateful for that.

I was halfway to Winnipeg when I heard God, as clear as that first day in the mud, he said, "I have called you to be a prophet."

*There's no such thing* was my instant rebuttal *the prophets are done away with!* Weren't they? I sure didn't see them around.

But in my head I was seeing things. God was showing me things about my life, fitting together pieces of a puzzle. I began to see glimpses of the life of a prophet even while I questioned: What was a prophet?

A prophet was a person God spoke to. A prophet had answers from God when no one else did. A prophet was really rejected. A prophet was a misfit, often without a home and completely at the mercy of God. They went where he wanted them to go and spoke when he wanted them to speak.

There in the truck God confirmed to me my calling. He had protected me from that tornado and He had a plan for me. I was just beginning to glimpse that plan and perhaps it was good that I didn't fully see it.

"Lord, I know you've begun a work in my life! I will do whatever you ask of me."

## CHAPTER THIRTY-SIX

# THE WARNING

I was walking down the street in Winnipeg one day when the Lord gave me a message for a minister who was in town.

I went to talk to him.

"Listen," I said. "The Lord has a message for you: you need to stop what you're doing and repent of your ways. Stealing. Using the Gospel for ill gain and for your own benefit. There is trouble ahead for you if you don't."

I didn't know what the trouble was, I just knew what the Lord had shown me. Something really bad would happen if this man did not heed what the Lord was telling him.

I left after delivering the message. I wanted to help him, to preach to him maybe, but I knew God simply wanted the message delivered.

For over a year the minister continued in his ways, travelling and preaching, using people and their money for his own gain.

One day I heard in the news that he had been killed: stabbed to death by his own son. My heart was heavy that day, knowing the prophecy had come to pass and that he had not taken heed to the Word of the Lord.

Another time I was driving my truck through Winnipeg and I was in a hurry. I was already late for a job I was doing and the heavy traffic wasn't helping the situation. Suddenly the Lord showed me there was a man I needed to talk to. I knew I was going to be late, but this was more important. I pulled the truck over and parked. There was a social event going on in the building where I had just pulled up next to. I went inside and waited for God to show me who he wanted me to speak to.

This was becoming a more common experience for me. The Lord would tell me he had a message for someone, and I would look for them. It's like the Lord would look through my eyes, and show me who I was supposed to talk to. My eyes would fasten on someone and then as I approached them He would give me the words to say! Never did I speak my own words. Never could I have made something like this up. That's why I always knew I was a nobody—everything I said to these people was from God—I just let him use my physical body to deliver the message.

Today was no different. As my eyes scanned the crowd, they fastened on a man and I walked over to him.

"Were you looking for a ride?" I asked.

He looked surprised. "Yes, actually. I need to be somewhere, but my ride never showed up."

"I can take you," I said. "Let's go."

He got into the truck and showed me where he needed to go. It was near where I was going anyway. As I drove, I spoke to him.

"I don't know you," I said. "But the Lord showed me he has a message for you. The Lord wants to restore back to you the salvation you once had, and by the time you get to your destination God's going to use you, and you'll going to be speaking to others about the goodness of God."

The man looked at me, totally amazed. He couldn't believe the words I had spoken. I let him off where he needed to go a few minutes later.

"Thank you," he said. "This means more to me than you know."

CHAPTER THIRTY-SEVEN

## ULTIMATUM

For ten years Lorraine and I had been a part of this church. They had become a family to me, and that was nothing to take lightly. I had been so young and naïve when I first began to go to church here. I had begged God to open His word to me, I had promised I would only preach the words He wanted me to preach, and God had been faithful! I was understanding so much of the Word, I was seeing the truths in the scripture, and much of what I was seeing did not match what John and the church were preaching.

Just last week John had asked me to counsel a new lady in the assembly. I was to tell her she could not wear jewelry and makeup. I was so conflicted inside. I knew that those things were not what God was about! They were earthly things of our outer body, our flesh, and God was interested in our heart, our inner man. I told John I couldn't do it.

Now John was after me again. He wanted me to counsel a couple where the man had been divorced and was now remarried. He had been married now for twenty years and was so happy in his marriage, but John wanted me to tell the man, according to the doctrines of the church, he had to leave this wife and go back to his first wife if he wanted to be right with God!

It made no sense to me. I knew that was *not* what the Word of God taught. God was not about keeping people in bondage. He was about setting the captives free. I felt that the doctrines of this church were keeping people in bondage and, the longer I stayed, the more conflict I felt in staying here. I could not keep my promise to God about preaching His Word as long as I remained in this church…but how could I leave John? We had grown very close in the past ten years together. We did everything together and we had become good friends. My whole life had been devoted to this church.

As much as the church was my family, God had shown himself to be my Father, and He held my full allegiance. I knew I wanted to spend my time learning more about God and striving to be like Him, instead of striving to be like the other pastors and ministers I had tried to copy in the past.

I had to leave.

Lorraine did not take the news well.

"How can you say you're leaving? You said this was the true church! You were the one who led us here and now you want to change?"

Darren, Michelle and Laura were playing in the living room and I saw Darren glance at us nervously, listening. I motioned Lorraine to follow me into the office and thankfully she complied.

"Lorraine, I didn't know the things I know now about the Bible when we first started going here. I was just learning. I see now that this church is not about the Word, but it is about what *men* want it to be. They have created their own teachings," I said, trying to explain my decision.

"I won't follow you—I'm warning you. If you leave, I'll stay here and I'm keeping the kids." Her eyes were dark and threatening.

"I can't stay, Lorraine. I have always put God first, you know that, and now is no different. I can't preach what the church teaches and stay true to God at the same time."

"Of course you can—this is the true church!"

"Okay," I said, "if this church is right and you believe in John—if John tells you to come with me when I leave, will you do that?"

She thought about it for a moment, her arms crossed tightly across her chest. Then she slowly nodded, "Yes, I would listen to him. But I know he won't ask me to go with you. He'll want me to stay."

I knew how strongly the church was against divorce. I was certain John would rather have Lorraine go with me and us both leave the church than for us to divorce just to keep her in the church.

That night Lorraine was quiet. She went to our room and I could hear her moving around in there a bit. When she came out she handed me an article from a newspaper. It was about a man in the States who had killed his wife and his children. "I'll do this," she said, her eyes dark and sinister, "just watch me."

I should have called the police then. They could have taken her to get help. But I didn't. Instead, I went to the church.

## CHAPTER THIRTY-EIGHT

# RIFT

The hardest thing, even after so many years, for me to talk about is Lorraine and the kids. The last thing I want to do is hurt anybody. But how can I tell my story without telling how things really were?

Soon after I married Lorraine I discovered that she had secrets. She would stay at home all the time and, when she was home, everything was dark, the curtains were always shut tight over the windows. She never liked to have people over to visit and she was never comfortable when we would go out with people. I was very social, so this was hard on me. Especially once I came to know the Lord. I would have people over to witness to or to have Bible studies with, and Lorraine hated that. There was a dark side to her that I didn't understand. I know now that she struggled with depression, and maybe other mental health problems, but at the time I just couldn't understand it.

There were really hard moments in our early years. Lorraine hated when I preached. She loved when I was discouraged because then she would come and pray for me! She liked that I could never speak in tongues and she could. When I would talk to people about the Lord, she would try to discredit me in front of the people and speak against me. She would try to manipulate me. She would plague me with guilt about not spending enough time with her and the kids, but when I would be there with her, she would be distant—and she would keep herself from me.

When I would go out to preach, sometimes Lorraine would threaten to kill herself. It would torment me—I'd be thinking about it the whole time I was supposed to be preaching! When I would come home I would creep into the house, looking around each corner scared I might find her body dead. I should have gotten help for her but I didn't know how and I couldn't understand how she could be this way. It just seemed like she was against me and everything I did. The closer I got to God, the harder she fought against me. She had been prophesied to about that very issue after a church meeting one night. Someone had come up to her and said, "If you fight God, sin lies at your door, and the devil will get a hold of your life." Well, the more she fought against me, the deeper into the darkness she seemed to fall.

Ever since God first touched me all I had wanted to do was preach, but I knew I couldn't preach and have my life be such a mess. I begged Lorraine to help me, to be on my side. I wanted desperately for us to be a united family, but I couldn't do that on my own! If she wasn't going to be with me there was no point in our marriage continuing this way.

## CHAPTER THIRTY-NINE

# WALKING AWAY

After that talk with Lorraine about leaving the church I set up a meeting with John and myself and our wives. This would not be easy, but I was willing to have the difficult conversation.

I sat forward in my chair and looked directly at John. "John, you know I love God."

John folded his hands coolly, "Of course you do! I've been with you nearly every step of the way, helping you find your way. I know you love God."

I know John liked to take credit for teaching me, and he *had* taught me a lot about the Bible in the beginning, but it was *God* who had shown me the Word, who had given me His Spirit and His wisdom in preaching and understanding.

I took a deep breath and continued, "John, I love God and have committed to preaching his Word." I looked up at him, searching his face for understanding. "I no longer feel comfortable with the teachings of this church. I have to move on."

John's face remained cool and complacent, like he was expecting this. "Art, we've talked about this before. You just need to give it time. This is the true church, but you're too excited right now. Eventually you will see this is the right way. These are the right teachings."

I shook my head, "I can't stay. That much is clear to me." I looked over at Lorraine and then began my next topic. "Lorraine has said she won't come with me if I leave."

The words hung in the air.

No one spoke so I continued. "I know if *you* tell her to, John, she'll listen to you. She will come with me."

John's face looked carved in stone. His eyes finally met mine in resolve. "I can't do that, Art."

"What do you mean?" I couldn't understand it. "Would you rather we get separated? You, who preach that divorce is the ultimate sin?"

John ignored my question and replied with one of his own, "Where would you take her? What are you going to do with no church—"

"She's *my* wife," I cut in, "not yours."

"I will not tell her to leave this church," he said.

"We're not leaving God," I said slowly, clearly, "just the church."

"I will not tell her to leave this church," he repeated.

I looked at Lorraine. She wore a smug smile as she quickly covered her mouth with her hand saying 'I told you so' with her expression. Nothing could have hurt more but, after this twisted conversation, I had never been more certain: this was not the right church.

I reached into my pocket and pulled out my minister's license. I had been so proud of this piece of paper. Now it felt heavy in my hands. I dropped it on the table in front of me.

"You can keep this," I said to John, "and you can keep her, too." I didn't even lift my hand to point to Lorraine. I felt too weak, too defeated. I just walked out of the meeting, out of the room and into a darkness so complete I didn't think I would ever come out of it.

## CHAPTER FORTY

## BETRAYAL

When I left that meeting with John and Lorraine I felt as if my life was over. All I had strived for with God, all the hope and visions I'd had for the future, preaching and serving God, it all felt impossible now. Lorraine would not go with me and I couldn't stay. So where did that leave me? And what about my children? I couldn't even bear to think about leaving them. What was I going to do?

I started by moving in with my sister in Winnipeg. I hated being away from home. I had given up the house to Lorraine but, in doing so, I'd left everything familiar to me: all my tools in the garage. I used to work in my garage for hours a day, and now I didn't have access to it. My room, my bed, my office—everything was gone. I felt so lost.

Worst of all was my kids. I hated not being a part of their lives. It tore at me to think that they might be thinking badly of me. I wanted them to know how much I loved them, how much I ached for them. This wasn't how I wanted things to be!

I had quit preaching in the church. How could I preach now that I was separated from my wife? I felt so alone, it was unbelievable. I was in such a dark place. I couldn't believe my life had come to this. I'd been through hardships before and I'd always been resilient, but the pain this separation cost me—it was almost too much to bear. I had finally found a family, not only a wife and children, but a family of believers who had been my friends and supporters. They had admired me and encouraged me and been there for me in every part of my life since I had met them, but now that I'd left my wife they were nowhere to be found. The family that I had come to love and depend on didn't even try to help me. They abandoned me. John, whom I had spent the better part of the last ten years with, hardly spoke to me anymore. It couldn't have hurt more if they had just beaten me and left me for dead. I felt so betrayed.

Not only that, but my business had hit rock bottom. I'd trusted my company with someone I thought would benefit me, an engineer. I'd considered myself lucky to have met him and been in business with him, but now he'd messed up a job and it had cost me everything. I had to sell my machinery just to cover the costs of the job he wrecked. Now I had no way of saving face. My company had lost trust with our clients, and no more work was coming in—and if it was, I didn't have the equipment to get it done! The only saving grace I had was the patent I was working on. It was always in the back of my mind but at the moment I couldn't use it. The patent wasn't finalized yet.

There were rumours going around that I had a girlfriend. I didn't care what the rumours were, but I just wished people would actually address the problem, confront me, and figure out for themselves what was going on!

I had in fact met a woman. I had told Lorraine I would find someone else if she wasn't going to be my wife anymore. I wasn't trying to hide it. It just bothered me that the church was okay with talking about it and gossiping about me but no one bothered to come see if I was ok or if the rumours were true!

A knock at the door startled me out of my thoughts.

"Can we come in?" There at the door stood two leaders of the church.

I shrugged and opened the door. They came in cautiously, looking around as if trying to find something. "What is it you'd like to know?" I asked. I knew they weren't here to help me.

They looked uncomfortable. "Well…we've been sent here to ask if you've been seeing anyone."

I stood there defiantly, upset that they had come in this manner, like two spies. "I see lots of people," I said, "what does it matter?"

"Well," they coughed and scratched and looked anywhere but at me. They weren't here to help me at all. They were just looking for a reason to get rid of me, to not be associated with me anymore. "We need to know if you have a girlfriend?"

"I have lots of girlfriends," I crossed my arms, "I have boyfriends too. What are you trying to say?"

But they wouldn't be direct. I wanted them to confront me, to ask if I was involved with another woman while I was still married. I wanted them to be real with me, so I could tell them what I was going through and then they could help me. But they didn't care about any of that. They just wanted to know if I had a girlfriend so they could have a reason to disfellowship me. They beat around the bush for a while and finally left with a veiled threat, "We will bring the head pastor here tomorrow. Will you have the same answers for him?"

"If he has the same questions, of course I will have the same answers." They left and I closed the door behind them. I felt terrible. The church had turned against me. I felt physically sick, but I knew I wasn't like them. I wasn't satisfied with just being a part of a religion. I wanted God, not doctrines and laws. And God had shown himself to me. And I knew God did not have a religion.

The next night they returned with their minister. I knew him and had worked with him before, but now he stood before me like a stranger. Like I was his enemy.

"We have heard enough, Art," he said, sitting on the sofa across from me. "We have no choice but to disfellowship you."

I was breaking there in front of them. I had admitted my faults, I needed their help. "Jesus left the ninety-nine for the one lost sheep," I said, leaning forward and pleading, "if you believe that I am lost, you should try to help me and win me back, not kick me out."

The minister seemed to consider my words for a moment, I could see the emotions flit across his face. Pitty, confusion, fear, and resolve, one by one. Then his eyes met mine, "You have sinned against God and against the church—we have to retract your membership."

*Do you see*, I felt God say to me, *This is not my church*.

I turned into the couch and wept. Never had I been so broken, so utterly lost. I didn't know why their disfellowship hurt me so profoundly. I was the one who had decided to leave because I didn't believe their doctrines. But it was how they turned on me. I just wanted to do what was right but, they fought me, and now that I was down, it was like they were just gonna kick me some more. They were treating me like I was the bad guy—like I was unfit to be with them, where just two months ago I'd been treated like royalty in their presence, one of the prominent preachers! I had preached at the Tabernacle in Tennessee! There weren't many pastors who could say that. The betrayal stung.

The ministers were about to leave and, against my better judgement, I stopped them. I was so broken. I needed any help I could get. "Can you pray with me?" I asked, tears streaming down my cheeks. I was in agony.

The men looked at each other uncomfortably and knelt down beside me. The words they prayed were as empty and fake as the gesture they had made in coming here. They didn't want God to help me and they probably didn't think he *should* help me.

I sat there through their prayer and finally cried out, "*I am in agony, Lord! I'm a nobody! Have mercy on me.*" I turned away from them, my whole body heaving with the hurt and rejection I felt. They stood up and left the house leaving me, weeping and raw and wounded.

CHAPTER FORTY-ONE

## WE DON'T HAVE TO BE PERFECT

I was with a woman one day when she told me about her uncle that was dying of cancer. I felt instantly that I should pray for him—it's what I would have done not long ago when I was with the church—but now I had doubts. How could God use me when I was such a bad person? I had no church. I'd given up my minister's license. I wasn't with my wife anymore. And worse...I had a girlfriend. 'I'm a nobody,' I thought, 'God can't use me now.' I didn't pray for him.

A week later I heard he was worse. "My uncle has been sent home to die," the woman told me. She was obviously upset and crying.

This time I clearly felt God tell me *'Go pray for him'*. I still had the same questions: 'why would God use me?' but I knew he would, because he had said it and he would do it. That's how God worked. There was no doubt in me now that if I prayed for this man he would be healed.

"Call your aunt," I said to her. "Tell her *I have a man with me that said that God spoke to him, and God wants to heal your husband*. God is going to raise him up."

"Send him over," the Aunt said.

We went to Transcona to the aunt's house. She invited us in and walked to the back room where Bill had been sent to die.

The room was small and the bed took up most of the space. The woman and her aunt stood on one side of the bed and I stood at the foot of the bed. The room smelled of death but I wasn't afraid. Even if the man was already dead I had no doubts God would raise him up. God had sent me to pray for him and I would do it.

I began to talk to the man. I talked to him about Jesus, about being born again. After a while I moved from the foot of the bed to the side of him and I grabbed him by the hand and I called for the life to come back into that body. I saw a vision as I said the words: I saw booster cables—and it was as if I was the booster cables between man and God—I stood in the gap. He needed to be brought back to life.

And just like that he sat up and started crying. His wife hugged him and held him close. They were both crying. "Something started to turn in me as you were speaking," he said, " and then I felt something lifted from me. The cancer is gone."

If I had ever seen joy, that was it.

Now he could become a witness for Jesus Christ. He was so excited he told everyone he knew what had happened to him.

I left thinking, *'why would God use me to do that?'*

I was not perfect. But if we think we have to be perfect before God can use us, then he'll never use us.

A month or two later I was at a church meeting in Transcona when a man walked up to me and said, "Isn't it wonderful how God healed that man?"

"What man?" I asked.

"The man in Transcona."

"How do you know about it?"

"I live next door," he said.

"Oh really?"

I was thinking then, why would God use *me* for the healing of that man? I lived fifteen miles away. There was a Christian available right next door. I had thought that all Christians had that power. And they *should*. But I was the man that God called for the job that day.

CHAPTER FORTY-TWO

## BACK UP WHAT YOU BELIEVE

My sister-in-law invited me to a meeting in downtown Winnipeg one night, but I had worked late and I wasn't sure I would be able to make it. Still, my goal in life was to talk to people, to get them into the letter God had written to them. I wanted to be available for people and help them so I resolved to go to the meeting, even if I was only there at the end.

I was still dressed in my work clothes when I got to the meeting as I had come over right after finishing my job. Even though I had rushed, the meeting was almost over when I arrived. I peeked through the door and saw them praying, so I went back up to the foyer to wait. Maybe there would still be someone I could talk to.

Sure enough, a woman came out of the meeting and noticed me sitting there alone.

I watched her approach me, her Bible in hand.

"Are you a Christian?" she asked me.

"You tell me what a Christian is and I'll tell you if I am one." I had no desire to play her game.

"Well, it's someone who has a relationship with Jesus Christ."

"Do I need to have a relationship with Jesus?"

"Well, yes! He's so good!" Now she thought she had a chance to save me.

"What happens if I don't know Jesus?" I asked.

"You must know Jesus or you will end up in hell." Her face became very grave.

"Hell!" I said. "What is hell like?" I wanted her to explain what she believed.

She looked at me strangely now. *Everyone* knew what hell was like, didn't they? "It's a horrible place of fire and torment where your body will burn eternally."

"Well, I don't want to go there!" I said.

By this time I was surrounded by people coming out of the meeting.

"Tell me," I said, "where in the Bible does it say if I don't know Jesus I will go to hell?"

She looked uncertain suddenly as she opened her Bible. I saw her glance behind her at someone, as if looking for help. Everyone in the crowd started searching for the verses. Pages were flipping frantically and people were muttering, whispering, trying to find the verses.

"Look," I said, stopping them. "I'm a salesman. Did you know that?"

The lady looked up at me, slightly relieved that I was letting her off the hook.

"And before I ever agree to sell anything, I need to believe in the product I'm planning to sell. I make sure I know everything about the product before I go out selling it. Do you get what I'm saying?" There was compassion in my heart as I looked at her.

"How long have you been reading your Bible?" I asked the lady.

She looked away guiltily. "Twenty years," she said, "but not faithfully."

"Should I look on you as my role model?" I asked. "The first thing you tell me about the Bible you can't even support. Why would you be a role model? None of you are able to defend your beliefs." I turned my attention to the whole crowd around me. "Start finding out if what you believe is true and learn to support it with scripture. Then you can be an effective tool in witnessing."

Here I was, a 'bad person', kicked out of the church. They thought I was lost and needed saving, but I had shown them quickly who the lost ones were. Why were people so quick to believe what they are taught by men, and eager to pass it on, without ever once questioning it? People don't know that they don't know.

## CHAPTER FORTY-THREE

## THE COLDEST NIGHT

It was the dead of night on one of the coldest days on record, and my brother and I were driving a small tin-can car on an old logging road in the middle of the bush a hundred and twenty miles from home. We were heading to a logging camp I had never been to before on a Sunday night and chances were we were the only ones out here until morning. It had snowed heavily and the logging road hadn't been cleared yet so when we turned the car onto it we immediately began pushing snow. It wasn't long before the car stalled and we were stuck.

My brother looked over at me when the lights blinked off in the car. "What will we do now?"

I grew up in the bush and I knew the dangers of it—especially in the winter and especially at night—only a fool goes out into the bush at night....I also knew I was the older brother and I had to make a decision.

"You wait here," I said, "I'll get out and walk to the camp. It can't be more than four miles."

I had on two pairs of jeans (already stiff and cold), gloves and a toque. I never took a parka to the bush because you couldn't move in them when you were working. I pulled my toque down low over my ears. "I won't be gone long," I said.

I stepped out of the car and my booted foot sunk deep into the snow. " Don't come looking for me," I warned my brother, " just sit tight and wait for help."

I had faced many cold walks before and I knew if I kept up my pace I would be able to stay warm enough to get to the logging camp and get help. I had matches in my pocket if I needed to stop and make a fire to warm up.

I had gone maybe a mile before doubts started to set in. It was so cold. *Should I turn around?* The camp might be farther than I had thought. The directions we had received said the camp was about three miles down this trail...but what if they were wrong? Then again, the camp could be closer than I thought. It could be just around that next bend in the trees. I kept walking.

Another mile passed. I stopped and crouched down low, rubbing my legs and tucking my face under my collar. The cold was starting to get to me and fear was creeping in with it. Now that I wasn't walking I let my eyes dart around the darkness, searching for shadows in the trees. I didn't like being in the bush alone and I never went in without a gun. Now I felt bare and vulnerable. Every snap of a branch or whisper of wind through the trees set my heart racing.

On a night this cold a person could last an hour—maybe two—before hypothermia would set in. I knew I couldn't be far off. My legs felt completely frozen and I was afraid that even if I survived this night, I might lose my legs. *I'd rather die*, I thought, *than have my legs cut off.*

Maybe if I could start a fire now I could get some warmth back into my body. I fumbled with the matches in my pocket but I couldn't move my hands enough to pick them up, never mind light them!

I had waited too long.

I must have been walking for three hours now, and there was no end in sight. I could feel hypothermia setting in. My mind felt muddled and confused. My breathing had slowed and was coming out in shallow puffs of white. My movements were clumsy and I could not direct my steps well. I knew if I stopped walking I would be done.

*I should have turned around. I should have stopped earlier to make a fire. I should never have left the car.* These thoughts came with each step I took through the fallen snow. I was not a quitter. I was more stubborn than any other person I knew—but this was no longer a matter of will. *I'm going to die out here*, I thought. *There's no way I'll make it out of here unless God does something.*

I crouched down trying to gain any warmth I could from my freezing body. I just wanted to close my eyes and rest. Maybe I could just lie down in the snow for a moment...

A wolf howled in the distance and my eyes popped open. I jerked up to a standing position and kept walking. My eyes struggled to focus. Soft light flickered over the tree branches like northern lights, and I knew I was beginning to hallucinate now. How could northern lights show through the trees? Yet I could see them, glowing yellow against the darkness, bouncing and dancing off the snow in front of me.

"God." My numb lips struggled to form the word. No other sounds came. Just that word, that name. My Father. My hope. My deliverer. I knew he was all these things and more to me, yet my soul doubted. How could I make it out of here? I was miles away from shelter in the middle of the night. Lost. No one would be coming down this old trail tonight. I should have reached the bush camp hours ago, but somehow I had miscalculated. Now I was in the middle of the bush, alone, with no protection: no light, no weapon, no warmth. The animals were dangerous enough in this place, but at the moment, the cold was my biggest threat.

My steps faltered and I stumbled, trying to gain my balance. I leaned over and rested my hands on my legs.

Suddenly I was completely bathed in a bright white light. I tried to turn—and through my blurred vision I saw a truck coming towards me! I couldn't move, and I didn't want to.

I must have looked terrifying to a stranger driving through in the night, but this vehicle was my salvation and I would not let them pass without picking me up!

I stood there, stiff and frozen in the middle of the logging trail like a deer in headlights, my hands outstretched in front of me. "Stop!" My lips tried but failed to speak the words.

The truck slowed to a halt just in front of me. I could feel the heat of it, rumbling there in front of me, and smell the diesel and the exhaust puffing out from it.

"Art!" It was my brother, "Get in!"

Someone had found our stranded car and picked up my brother! He had brought them out here to find me. It was so impossible, yet it had happened. Someone else had been down this road in the middle of the night—I knew it was no coincidence. God had sent them out here to rescue us.

I had been saved, when I surely should have died.

## CHAPTER FORTY-FOUR

# THE PIT

The Bible talks about David being in a pit. So few people I feel know about being in a pit like David was. He says the pit was a horrible place and he cries for God to take him out of it but very little is written about it.

As much as I loved God, I had been doing things my way and I needed discipline. I was his child and he needed to correct my ways.

For six years I experienced that pit that David was in. I was under a curse. I had no money—couldn't buy or sell anything. Everything I put my hand to seemed to fail.

I knew things were bad. I wanted to be a better person but no matter what I did, I couldn't change myself. I was bad, and I was angry. I walked around like a man of rage. I'd tear a strip off of a person for looking at me the wrong way. I was vicious. People said I was backsliding or worse, that I'd become 'lukewarm.' They tried to hide their disapproving stares but I saw them. I felt so awful—guilty, so ugly inside—and hopeless.

Things with my kids were bad and that alone was enough to torment me. My soul ached in me. The pain I felt knowing my kids were hurting because of me was unbearable. I was in agony. I tried to do what I could for them. I had no money but, anything I could scrounge, I would use to make their lives better. I wanted them to have a good life!

What made everything worse was the woman I was dating. I knew I shouldn't be with her, but I couldn't be without her either. Such a little woman—I could have tossed her over a building if I wanted to—but she had power over me. She didn't have much interest in my kids and they didn't like her much either. We fought all the time. I would break up with her and then be so miserable within days I'd want her back. Our relationship went on for years like that. I was in bondage to her. I needed her.

Lorraine would use her against me and she wouldn't let me see the kids if my girlfriend was around. It tore me up inside.

I felt completely isolated and alone. The only way I could find relief was on my Harley Davidson. I'd start it up and drive as fast as I could until at last the roaring of the engine and the wind would drown out the noise of my own mind. I'd ride that motorcycle for hours, the wind whipping my face and hair, finally able to find some relief. I'd get home and drop into bed, exhausted. If I was lucky I'd fall asleep before my mind had time to torment me again. *Don't let me go, Lord*, I'd beg. I felt as if I were hanging on by a thread. *Don't let me go!*

Years had passed. Things hadn't changed and I was wearing out. I had come to a point where I could barely function. I stood in front of my door one evening, and my hand was shaking so badly I could barely get the key into the lock. That's when everything just broke for me. I leaned my head against the door, trying to calm myself enough to open the lock. "I can't do this anymore—I've let you have your way in my life, but now I'm asking you—let me out of this pit! Set me free!"

I knew God had been disciplining me. I had judged a Christian wrongly, when it wasn't my place to judge them. Who was I to say someone was good or bad? God had shown me a verse in Matthew saying *'agree with thine adversary quickly, while thou art in the way with him; lest at any time the adversary deliver thee to the judge, and the judge deliver thee to the officer, and thou be cast into prison, and you will not come out until you have paid the last mite.'*

I had hated someone who loved the Lord, and now I was paying the consequences. I had been doing things my own way and God was now taking the time to show me how to be His child. He was upset with me. What father doesn't chastise his children? The Bible says, *My son, despise not the chastening of the LORD; neither be weary of his correction* and I had endured his correction. I did not fight His chastisement, I knew I needed it. I had so much to learn, but I wasn't sure I could last much longer. The lock clicked open and I stumbled into the room, weary and broken. I dropped onto the bed and fell into a deep sleep.

That night I saw a vision. I was lying on my bed and a man walked into the room. He looked at me and said, "Art, come here." When I got to the door he was nowhere to be found. I went out into the hall. The stairs were gone and there was a long hallway in their place. I started to walk down the hallway and it was as if I were walking in a different realm. A gentle breeze was blowing and I began to feel light and refreshed. I leaned forward into the breeze and started running. It felt so *good*! Like nothing I had felt before. The wind was hitting my hair, I was running fast and I felt like I could keep going forever. I didn't want it to end!

The next morning I woke up thinking of the dream and what it could have meant.

Immediately I felt God say to me: *The wind is my presence. I will be taking you out of the pit.*

## One year later...

The room was dark except for a small desk lamp. I sat on the side of my bed staring out the window across from me. It looked directly out over a street corner where a yellow streetlight shone into the darkness. Snow fell softly through the halo of light the streetlamp created. It was the dead of night so the streets were quiet, no traffic, no sirens. A year had passed since I had had the vision of being set free from this pit, yet nothing had changed. It was Christmas and I couldn't be with my family, but I couldn't be with God either.

"Lord," I said into the stillness, "why don't you let me go?"

I had come to the end of me—there was nothing left.

One week later I was sitting on my bed and all of a sudden a five hundred pound weight lifted from my shoulders. The tormentor had left and I knew I was out! I didn't have to guess. When someone puts you in a chokehold and finally lets you go, you know it!

I felt new energy. My mind felt free. I had business ideas again. I had ambition. I felt like I could do anything now!

"Just watch me," I told people.

I was out of the pit and nothing could stop me now.

CHAPTER FORTY-FIVE

# BALANCING ACCOUNTS

I was walking down the street in St. Boniface one day when I noticed a man walking towards me. He was big and tough looking and it seemed like he was coming right for me. I was sure I had never seen him before.

"Hey," the man stopped in front of me. "Are you Arthur Adam?"

How did he know my name? "Yes, why?"

He held up a folded newspaper. "You're in the paper. Someone's trying to get in contact with you."

"Really? Who?" I was still trying to figure out how this guy knew me and what he wanted.

"Some company owes you money, I think." He handed me the paper. "Here, let me show you." He opened the paper to page five and, sure enough, there was my name along with the name of a law firm: "*Notice to Arthur Adam and Atlas Utilities contractor. We are holding some money for you and you have until the end of this month to pick it up.*"

I went straight to the law firm and picked up my money.

I had done some work for a company while I was in the pit but they had gone bankrupt and I hadn't been paid. Now, more than five years later, the money was coming back to me. I couldn't believe I was getting this money! I was broke—I had nothing to my name. If that man would not have shown me the paper, I never would have known to get the money. Could this man have been an angel?

After that, things began to change in my life. My patent went through and I could start pushing pipe again using my new machine. I started getting big jobs and contracts. I purchased apartment blocks and began getting income from that direction as well. Money I had lost in the pit came flowing back to me abundantly.

It wasn't long after that, as I was installing a 42 inch culvert across a highway outside of Winnipeg, two men approached me. They were wearing suits and fancy shoes and I guessed they were part of the workplace safety board or something similar as I hardly ever wore proper safety gear on the job site. Even now I didn't have a vest or hard hat on. I scrambled up out of the hole I was working in.

"Can I help you?" I asked.

"Are you Arthur Adam?"

"Call me Adam," I said, nodding and eyeing them carefully.

"Ok, Adam, we've got a job if you're interested. You've been recommended to us and there's no other company around here that can do it."

"What kind of job?" I asked.

"We need you out at the airport. It's a big job, putting pipe under the runways."

Now I was interested. I knew I could do the job.

"I can do it" I said.

"How will you do it?" they asked.

"I won't tell you," I said. My method was simple and I knew if I told them they would just find someone else to do the same thing. They wouldn't need me.

"You want us to hire you without knowing how you will get the job done?"

I shrugged. "I'll get the job done."

They talked quietly between themselves for a minute and finally turned back to me.

"You're scaring me," the one guy said, "but we sure need this done. You're hired." They shook my hand, gave me their card, and disappeared.

The money I made on that job alone was more than I could have imagined. God would continue to provide for me, over and over again.

Another time during the pit I had lost three hundred thousand dollars to a group of men that had put their houses up for collateral on a deal we had made. Well, the deal fell through on their end and they couldn't pay, but I let them keep their houses and took the short on the money.

Now suddenly I had a man approach me who wanted shares in my patented machine. He bought three hundred thousand dollars worth and then found out he couldn't keep the shares because of a conflict of interest with another company he was involved in. He told me to keep the money. He would just bow out as a shareholder. I couldn't believe how clear it was that God was repaying me for what had been lost, right to the last cent.

CHAPTER FORTY-SIX

# PREPARATION

For several years I continued with my business, Adam's Underground. Things were going well and I was thriving financially. I bought a big house on Dawson Road and that gave me a couple of acres to work on. It felt good to finally have a place of my own again. I even got a dog, a big German Shepherd that would greet me every day when I got home from work.

I still missed my kids like crazy. They would come over to visit sometimes, and we'd go for a drive, or out to St. Labre to spend time with my family. All of my children were involved with music in some way or another. I'd made sure to pay for lessons if they wanted them, and now they often sang and performed at different church events or programs. I'd go to all the events and proudly watch them. I bought a good camera so that I could video tape them performing.

At Darren's high school graduation, I showed up a bit late. The place was packed and there was no way I was going to get a good seat. I went up to someone who seemed to be in charge and told him I was supposed to film the event for the school. He quickly moved two women out of the front row, apologizing to me for not being aware of this, and let me set up my camera equipment with the best seat in the house. Darren looked surprised when he saw me there in the front row, and his somewhat embarrassed, but happy smile made me glow with pride.

One fall I was tossing hay bales onto my pickup with one of my workers when I felt a sudden sharp pain in my neck. It was the worst pain I had ever felt, like every muscle from my neck down my spine had seized up and was spasming. Two fingers in my hand were numb and I knew there must be a pinched nerve somewhere. The pain was excruciating. The guy I was working with took me to the hospital and I ended up being given some pain pills and told to take some time off for a while. Rest would be the only cure.

Rest for me was nearly impossible. I felt panicked inside. I was someone who loved to be busy. I got home and went to lie down, but even when I lay down there was no relief. It seemed the only way I could cope was by walking.

The pain was so bad that in the next seven days I slept only about ten hours. I was up all night and all day. If someone had come to rob my place in the middle of the night I'd have known about it. I'd try to sleep in a chair and, the minute I'd doze off, it was like a trigger and the pain would shoot through me again. The nerves in my neck were so tight I couldn't move it at all without enormous pain. I went to see a chiropractor and when he tried to twist my neck I threatened to pick him up by the leg and smash him against the building—I was so sensitive. This was the worst pain I had ever experienced in my life.

Days turned into weeks and weeks into months and I was totally incapacitated. I knew now God was trying to get my attention. I had been so busy with work I realized that I had lost focus on what really mattered. I began to study and, now that my attention was fully turned on God, amazing things started to happen.

I remember kneeling on my floor in the living room one night, worshipping God, singing to him and telling him from my deepest self how much I loved him.

"Heavenly Father, I appreciate you…" I sang the words, but my mind was on God, how thankful I was for what He had done in my life. "Heavenly Father I appreciate you…" How he had come to me and made himself real to me. "I love you, adore you. I bow down before you…" He was everything to me, my Father, my comforter, my provider, my friend. I desired him above all else in this world.

I was focused on these things and singing to God when suddenly His presence fell upon me. It was so strong I felt a fear unlike anything I had ever felt before. The glory of God filled the room and I was sure if I turned around to see Him I would die. That's how real it felt.

I knelt there in the presence of God and I worshipped Him. I had built an altar of worship to God and He had shown up.

This was a new page in my life—a completely new experience God was bringing me into. It was as if my physical eyes were closed and God was opening my spiritual eyes. Even when I drove my vehicle the presence of God would come upon me and I would pull over and stop my truck to stay in that presence. When He's right there—you need to stay there! It was like I was captured, my mind one hundred percent focused on the Word. I would get up each morning and talk to the Lord, I'd go to work and scripture would be running through my mind. I would get home and I couldn't wait to spend time with the Lord. I had spiritual experiences that I can't even begin to speak of: things God would show me, places He would take me in the Spirit.

He opened my ears one night and I was hearing conversations people were having in their house miles away from me, and when I told them about it they couldn't believe what I was saying! How had I heard them? How could I possibly know what they had been saying?

I would ask God, 'why are you showing me these things?' I didn't understand! But it was for my learning. I would be with the Lord late into the night and when I would go to sleep verses would run through my mind all night long.

I had stacks of notes and messages. So many I couldn't begin to count them.

"Why are you giving me these messages when I have no church? I have no one to give these messages to," I would ask.

Still He taught me. I became a man mighty in scripture. The Word was constantly in my heart and on my mind. I was captivated by God and, I didn't understand it yet, but God was preparing His church for me at the same time as He was preparing me for His church.

## CHAPTER FORTY-SEVEN

## TWO CRIES FROM THE HEART

**Adam**

I'd been in Winnipeg over twenty years now. I had retired from my business (Adam's Underground) and sold it, and now I was becoming bored. It was time for me to try my hand at something else. I bought a slasher and headed northwest to Cowan to work in the bush with one of my brothers.

I was lonely. It seemed like I could never find a woman who was good for me, and who loved the Lord.

I was driving my truck to Swan River to get some equipment for the bush and I remember praying to God, '*Lord, find me someone that will work with me, a companion, someone who loves you so we can serve you together.*' I'd made a mess of my relationships. Every time I tried to find someone, it never worked out right because I had been looking for what *I* wanted, but it wasn't what I needed. Now I was asking God for help because I didn't like to be alone, but I couldn't be with someone who didn't believe like I did. It was a sincere request and God knows the heart. He doesn't always give us what we want, but He gives us what we need.

Little did I know on the other side of the mountain God was already at work with my request...

# Edie

It was late summer and I was a mess. I'd wanted to take my kids camping this weekend, but my husband and his *girlfriend* (I still couldn't think of her without wanting to spit) were taking *my kids* on holiday instead. This had been the longest, hardest year of my life, and I felt like I was being eaten alive from the inside. I was so hurt and angry. Not only had my husband gotten a girlfriend and left me, he'd somehow convinced my two kids to come with him! I was left alone with a big farmhouse I couldn't afford and paying alimony for my kids that I couldn't live with. I felt so betrayed. To top it all off my dad had just passed away. Now I'd found out I couldn't take my own kids camping.

I slammed the door to my house shut with the last load of camping gear in my arms. I certainly wasn't going to sit at home and pout. I shoved the gear into the trunk of my car. I'd go camping alone if I had to. I hitched the small camper to my car, cranked up the stereo, and tore down the driveway like I was being chased. In a way--I was.

Driving fast made me feel like I was getting somewhere. I watched the farmhouse fade away in my rear view mirror and felt a grip on my chest slowly ease up. I pressed harder on the accelerator and sped down the highway at top speed. People must have thought I was a maniac driving the way I did, but I didn't care. At this point, I almost welcomed the thought of an accident. A car wreck would match how I felt inside. Mangled. Sometimes I wondered if someone might come over one day and find me hanging in the garage.

I got to the lake within an hour. It was one my family and I had visited often in my childhood, and the familiar landscape brought memories flooding back to me: summers swimming in the cold lake, catching minnows with little white nets, playing volleyball in the hot sand, and building sand castles. Memories of my kids chasing fireflies, or roasting hotdogs over the campfire. All the memories were good ones, but they still brought pain to my heart. How had my life ended up this way? I'd always tried to be good, to do the right things, but it never seemed to work out.

I parked my car, set up the camper, and decided to go for a bike ride down a road I used to bike down as a kid. It was old and closed down now, but it used to lead down to an old Bible camp I had attended as a child.

I wasn't anywhere with God. I had no faith. I'd grown up in a traditional Baptist church, gone to church every Sunday, attended youth group as a teen and even joined the church choir. To me it was just a place to go, to meet people to hang out with. Now I saw it was just a social club. Too many people just went to church to see who was there, what they were wearing, and maybe go out for lunch afterwards. Everyone loved a good gossip session too, and now I was suffering the brunt of that.

When my marriage had first started to fall apart I had gone to the church to seek help. I had been devastated, but no one had stopped to help me. I was left sitting alone in the pew wondering what was wrong with me and what would become of me. I talked to the minister, but he couldn't help me. His advice had been to get back together with my husband, so he could help us together. *'My husband won't leave his girlfriend'* I had answered. There was no working around it—my marriage was through.

I was pedalling my bike hard, not taking time to enjoy the scenery around me, just going as fast as I could, pushing myself, always running, because if I stopped I might not ever start again.

I got to the end of the road and dropped to the ground— it was the end of the road in my life too—I was finished.

"*God!*" I cried out to the Lord from deep inside of me, "*I need help! I have no hope!*" My whole body was heaving with the emotion I felt. This was my last resort. If God didn't help me, I would be lost. I sat there alone and cried, letting all my pent up anger and hurt pour out of me as I watched the last of the sun sink beneath the horizon. "*You have to help me, Lord...*"

CHAPTER FORTY-EIGHT

## MEETING EDIE

Adam
The first time I met Edith was not a coincidence. Once a month I went to Winnipeg to do business and usually it was on a Friday night. I was coming down the hill in my truck when I approached the intersection and realized I needed to fill up with gas. I always carry a big slip tank of fuel in the truck so I pulled my truck over and started to fill my tank. God had stopped me there, because he wanted Edith to catch up with me. I was on the phone as I filled up my tank but, as I was talking, I saw another car pull up beside me at the intersection. They were gone again before I was finished.

Meanwhile Edith was in that car that stopped beside me. She was with another woman and when they stopped at the stop sign Edith saw my truck said 'Adam's Underground' and she was curious, because she was the accountant for Spruce Products and I was a contractor for them. She made my checks! I finished with the gas and then took off, but again I decided to stop first at Chicken Chef to grab a coffee.

When I pulled into the Chicken Chef, Edith's car was there too. They had been getting a coffee as well. I bumped into the lady she was riding with and I knew her. She introduced me to Edith and that was the very first time we met.

I didn't think anything of that first encounter with Edie and I didn't see her again until just before Christmas.

I had driven in to Spruce Products to pick up my check and she was just arriving there from picking up the mail. I still remember the red jacket she wore and her long dark curly hair.

She came up to greet me like we were old friends. "Hi!" she said. "Beautiful day, isn't it?"

"Sure," I was never shy around women, but suddenly I wasn't sure what to say. "I'm here for my check."

"Oh yeah, come on in and I'll get it for you." I followed her inside and she was back in no time with my check.

We exchanged a few more words and then, for some reason, I found myself saying, "You should let me take you out for coffee sometime."

She looked surprised. "Okay," she said. "You know where to find me."

"Yeah," I turned and headed for the door.

"It was nice seeing you again, Arthur."

"Call me Adam."

I jumped into my truck and drove off.

# Edie

It was the longest Christmas of my life. I tried to keep busy, but over the holidays everybody had their own plans and agendas, and I had none. I had rented out my farm house and my land, and gotten a little blue house next to Spruce Products where I worked. Even though I wasn't surrounded by the haunting memories of my family in the old farm house, being in this new house felt just as empty. It wasn't home. I spent most of the holiday shut inside my house, alone, reading and watching television. Focusing on the small day to day tasks made it easier to forget the bigger problems I was surrounded with: like what I was going to do with my farm, how could I have full custody of both my children, and how empty I felt all the time.

I found myself thinking about Adam. I had heard a lot about Adam from my friend, how he used to be a pastor but now he was just working in the bush. How he talked about his God all the time, but he never seemed religious. He had said he would call me…but what was I thinking? Why would he be interested in a woman like me? My life was a total mess. Still…I hoped he would call.

# Adam

Work got busy and I didn't call Edith. Christmas and the new year came and went, and finally I said to myself either I would call her or I wouldn't, but I needed to decide now what to do.

I called her up that evening and invited her to dinner.

She accepted.

Our first date I picked her up in my truck and we went to the local hotel restaurant. I wanted to make a good impression, but I didn't want to do anything too fancy either. I was just looking to get to know her better. She sure looked pretty all dressed up and I was surprised by how much I wanted to impress her. I helped her out of the truck and into the restaurant and, from there on, the date went downhill. The service at the restaurant was terrible, but since I was trying to be so nice and polite because it was our first date, I didn't complain or tell the waitress how bad it was.

Edie was nice—she thought I was funny, and I thought she was kind, but as we were leaving the restaurant I saw her stiffen at something. There in the foyer of the hotel was a sign announcing the wedding of her ex-husband and his girlfriend. The wedding was taking place this very night at this very hotel, just in a different room, and she hadn't known about it. She didn't yell. She didn't cry. She just turned to me and said, "You can take me home now, please."

I felt so terrible for her. I could imagine what she must be going through and I didn't envy it.

## Edie

"Edie, you need to take a holiday!" my cousin told me one day in late January. "You should come with me to Mexico for two weeks. I've found a great deal and I would love it if you came with me."

It sounded heavenly. I would have given almost anything to just get away at that point, so it didn't take much convincing from my cousin for me to book a flight and come with her. I told Adam about the trip the next time I ran into him.

"Hey, that will be nice," he said to me.

I knew he made monthly trips to Winnipeg for business, so I suggested, "Hey, it would be nice if you were in Winnipeg on the day I get back so I could get a ride back to Swan River with you."

He seemed non-committal and shrugged.

"Well, if it was on the same day," he said, "I could probably come pick you up."

"Okay," I nodded and smiled, but I knew by his expression and the fact that he didn't ask for any of my flight information that he probably wouldn't come. Still, I hoped he would. I tried not to get my hopes up and just focus on the trip and enjoy the time away from the cold and the troubles of my home life.

## Adam

I knew I would pick her up. I knew the moment she asked me—I would have done anything she asked, and not because I wanted to please her, but because I wanted to be good to her. She deserved someone in her life to show mercy to her for once, and maybe I was the man for the job. She needed help in her life and I would help her, but I didn't want to be in a serious relationship unless I knew the woman loved God and put Him first above all else. Edith was not at that point. Still, I knew God wanted me to show mercy to her, and there was something in me already that felt compassion towards her. I called her house while she was gone and talked to her daughter, Pam, to get the flight information.

The snow storm came on suddenly and with a fierceness I had rarely seen before. I made it into Winnipeg but I could tell this storm wasn't going anywhere. I parked the car I was driving and went into the airport to wait for Edith. I couldn't wait to see the expression on her face when she saw me waiting there for her.

I bought a coffee and went to sit on a bench next to the arrival gate. People were coming off a flight already, looking tanned and a bit depressed. I bet they weren't too happy to have left the Mexican beaches and ended up back in a snowstorm in Winnipeg.

Suddenly Edith was there at the top of the escalator. She looked good. Her curly hair was pulled back and I could see some shiny earrings she must have bought in Mexico. Her eyes were scanning the crowd and I stood up to signal her I was here. Her face lit up in a smile and she gave an excited wave—boy, did her eyes sparkle when she smiled.

"You came!" she said, coming to greet me when she got through the gate. I gave her a hug—she still smelled a bit like sun lotion and salt water.

"Of course," I shrugged. "I was coming to Winnipeg today anyway, so it just worked out."

She must have known that to be a lie when she saw the ferocity of the storm as we stepped out of the airport and tried to find the car in the blinding wind and snow.

"You drove here in *this!*" she exclaimed, shivering and pulling her jacket tightly around her.

I swung her luggage into the trunk and opened the passenger door for her.

"Well, it wasn't this bad when I left this morning." She looked at me over the top of the car and I knew I was caught. We both laughed. "Hey, do you want a ride or what?"

We got into the car and started the long ride home.

She told me about her trip, we listened to music on the radio and chatted in between songs, but the storm was getting worse the whole drive west. I had just made it past Portage La Prairie when the highway we had been on was shut down. I could barely see a foot in front of me and the wind was blowing hard. Luckily the roads weren't that icy yet, but I knew that it wouldn't take long for these prairie winds to polish the snow like glass. I hadn't noticed, but Edith had become quiet beside me. I glanced over at her, she was scowling out the window looking deep in thought.

"Hey," I said. "Tell me about your walk with the Lord."

She looked over at me. "What walk?" She shrugged and looked back out the window, "I don't even know if God is real. I'm on the fence about it."

I waited for her to continue.

"My Opa loved the Lord," she said, as if remembering him from a dream, "I remember him praying, talking to God like he knew him…" She looked back at me and there were tears in her eyes. "But I've never experienced God like that. All I've seen is church and religion, and I'm through with that stuff."

I was proud of her for admitting that to me. She was honest and I appreciated that.

"Me, I've seen a lot of religion too," I said, "And I'll tell you a lot of that stuff is just people trying to control other people."

I saw her nod and I knew she was listening. "But *God* is real. And I'll tell you something else, God has sent me to help you."

The rest of that ride I was able to tell Edith about my experience with the Lord. How He had made Himself real to me, the miracles He had done in my life, and she listened hungrily.

I know God kept us safe through that storm, and it seemed like in no time we were back at her little blue house even though it had been over three hundred miles of driving through that storm.

"Thanks Adam," she said when I dropped her off, "for the ride, and for the company. I'll think about what you've said…"

"Good night."

I watched her walk into her house and shut the door. Then I turned around and drove back into the storm to my house in Cowan.

CHAPTER FORTY-NINE

## GOD TOUCHES EDIE

**Edie**

Adam continued to work in the bush, and on my days off sometimes I would go with him. I'd sit in the slasher and watch as he stacked and cut the wood like it's what he'd been doing his whole life. He seemed at home in the bush. The more time I spent with him, the more I found myself drawn to him, and to the wisdom he had. I was so tired of phony people, and Adam might have been rough around the edges, but he was real—and he talked about his God as if He were real too. I hadn't met anyone like him before.

We began to spend a lot of time together. When he wasn't working, he'd come to my place and we'd sit in the back of my garage where a small wood stove stood. We filled the garage with wood and then he'd light the fire and sit and smoke and we'd talk for hours like that. Once he'd start talking it was hard for him to stop. I'd laugh and say "time out! I need a break!" But I always wanted more. I was like a sponge soaking up everything he was teaching me. I began to see things about the Word of God, things the church had never taught me. I started seeing the difference between religion and true belief, and that the two didn't necessarily go hand in hand. Adam lived what he believed, and it showed in everything he did. He loved the Lord, and I was starting to see I hadn't even had a glimpse of what that love could be like.

We weren't officially dating—Adam had never really asked me to be his girlfriend, and I was enjoying our time together so much I never wanted to rock the boat by asking him to define our relationship. Every so often though, I would wonder if maybe he was seeing someone else.

One Saturday in early spring I had gone out to run some errands. Adam was in Winnipeg on one of his monthly trips, and I couldn't help feeling slightly upset that he never invited me along, or even told me about what he was up to. I was so focused on these thoughts that I didn't even see his blue truck parked by the garage when I drove home. I was shocked when I heard the lawn mower running, and went into the backyard to see what was going on.

There was Adam dressed in work clothes and mowing my grass. That wasn't all he had done. I could tell—all the yard work that early spring requires was underway. My yard was big, and full of large overgrown trees. He had trimmed some and there was already a pile of dead branches burning off in the back. A garden plot was tilled and warming in the sunshine.

I felt tears fill my eyes, and deep gratitude overwhelmed me. Never had anyone treated me the way Adam did.

## Adam

I'll never forget the look on Edith's face when she came home from her errands that Saturday and found me working in her yard. She looked shocked and pleased, and so pretty in her spring dress. She didn't know what to say. Here she thought maybe I was in Winnipeg with another woman, but the whole time I had been at her place working in her yard.

She made me lunch, and as I sat at her table she turned to me and said, "Why are you so kind to me?"

"The Lord has told me to show mercy to you," I said. Then I told her the story about David and Saul. How after David had become king, he sought out any survivors of Saul's family because he wanted to help them, even though Saul had spent much of his life trying to kill David. The only survivor was a crippled boy, who had been injured when he was just a baby and was unable to walk. David showed mercy to that boy, and took him into the palace and treated him as if he were family. That's the mercy God has towards us. We are weak and crippled, undeserving of his mercy, but he invites us into his family and treats us as his very own. God had done that for me, and I had that same compassion towards Edith.

After that talk, things changed between us. I knew that God wanted to work in Edith's life. He began to show me things about her, truths that only she knew—but now God was showing me. I would speak them to her, and it wasn't easy. It's hard to tell someone the truth about the dark secrets of their life. Edith wanted to keep them hidden—especially from me—but God was showing them to me to make Himself real to her. We need to prove to ourselves whether God is real or not.

One day after I spoke to her about something God had shown me she jumped up off the couch, "How can you possibly know that?" She was visibly upset and yet astonished.

## Edie

When Adam first started telling me things about myself nobody knew I felt like the woman at the well in John four, in the Bible. How could Adam possibly know these deep dark secrets that I had? God was shaking me. He was waking me up to show me my true self. We can never truly repent until we see ourselves truly. I had been in darkness, unaware of how much sin was in my life. It's amazing how we can be in such a bad state but still deep down we think we are good. We convince ourselves we are good and it takes God to show us otherwise.

Never once did Adam tell me I needed to be saved. Never once did he tell me to change, to try and be better, to give my heart to the Lord. He just talked. He listened to what God wanted him to say and he would say it. Finally I had had enough.

It was a sunny summer morning, July thirteenth—I'll never forget the date. Adam and I were sitting on the front steps of my house and it was hot. I still remember the way the sun was beating down on me.

Adam had told me a story that reflected exactly how I felt. He said he had gone fishing one day with his son Darren. They had been crossing a river on some stones when Darren had fallen into the water. His expression as he surfaced in the water and raised his hand out was *'if my Dad can only grab me I'll be safe.'* Such was his confidence in his Dad.

I cried when I heard that story. Darren knew his Father would help him when he was in trouble—and that's exactly how Adam viewed God. I wanted that desperately: to know my God was real, to know that when I was in trouble if I could just reach up my hand my heavenly Father would save me!

"I want what you have," I said to Adam. "All my life I've had religion and it's been empty. The God you serve is real—he speaks to you and I want that God."

"I'm going to pray for you," Adam said.

When I heard those words, I knew this was God. Adam had never prayed for me before. This wasn't something we were doing because we wanted to be good or do the right thing. This was God drawing me—He had sent Adam to me for just this purpose.

"It's hot here. Let's go to the backyard," Adam said, standing up and leading me to a table and chairs that were set up in the shade under a big tree behind my house. I sat down in the chair. I wasn't really sure what I was supposed to do.

Adam began to pray. I had never heard anyone talk to God the way he did. He asked the Lord to put my sins away into the farthest corner and to give me a white robe of righteousness. Then he touched my face and I felt a lightning bolt go right through my body.

I jumped up and grabbed on to the table. "Adam! You won't believe what is going through my body." I felt electricity from the top of my head to my toes.

"That's God," Adam said. "You needed that experience to know that God is real."

Even though I had been in church all my life I had never experienced God like that. It was like everything happened at once for me in that moment. I had been carrying around a load of self-condemnation—and it was gone—it had been lifted off my shoulders. I received the Holy Spirit—I felt him course through me like lightning, and I had been delivered of spirits at the same time.

That was my first encounter with God and I knew I would hold on to that forever. I felt so clean—like I was wearing a white robe of righteousness, and all my own filthy sins were gone. The old Edie died that day. I was a new creature! The God Adam served was my God now too and I would forever love Him for touching me that day and beginning this new work in me.

I was so exhausted after that when Adam suggested we go for a drive, I fell asleep in the truck and slept through the whole ride.

CHAPTER FIFTY

## BAPTISM

**Adam**

The change in Edith was something to behold. Her whole demeanour had changed—she was a new creature. When you receive salvation, you receive the forgiveness of sin, healing, and deliverance. It truly changes your life. What a joy it was to see a baby in the Lord—how full of joy they are, and how fresh and simple their belief is. It reminded me of my first experience with the lady telling me about how experiencing God is like tasting a cheeseburger, and how I had prayed and felt that new life in me! What a feeling that is when God first touches your life! Just as God had begun a work in Edith, it was only the beginning. He wasn't finished with her yet.

I was in Winnipeg one day when the Lord showed me something about Edith. I called her.

"Hello?" She picked up the phone on the first ring.

"Hi, it's Adam," I began.

"Oh, hi!"

"Listen, the Lord has shown me something—and I want Him to show it to *you*. Ask Him to show you what is displeasing to Him in you."

### Edie

After Adam called me I went into my room. I knew the Lord talked to Adam, and I wanted Him to talk to me too, and I knew that

He would. I sat down on my bed and just talked to the Lord, thanking Him for what he'd already done in me, and asking Him to search me and show me what He had shown Adam.

While I was praying, three thoughts came to my mind and I knew they were from God. They were personal—the first two were about my character, things that needed to change in me. The last thought I didn't quite understand, it wasn't about my character at all, it was just a word, a picture—but it stuck with me. I shared the first two with Adam but I kept the third one a secret. I didn't understand it yet and I didn't want to talk about it. He didn't seem impressed with what I told him though—he was searching for something and that wasn't it. The third thought kept coming back to me though, so I finally told Adam what it was.

"That's it!" He said, "That's what God told me."

He confirmed what the Lord had shown me—that it was a spirit in me I needed to be delivered from. The verse he showed me was Luke 11:24-26 *"When the unclean spirit is gone out of a man, he walketh through dry places, seeking rest; and finding none, he saith, I will return unto my house whence I came out. And when he cometh, he findeth it swept and garnished. Then goeth he, and taketh to him seven other spirits more wicked than himself; and they enter in, and dwell there: and the last state of that man is worse than the first."*

"You're a believer now," he said to me, "you have the authority in Christ to tell that spirit to leave."

I went to work the next day and something started to happen to me. I just wasn't myself. I felt panicked and shaky, my mind was scrambled, I couldn't focus on anything. I told my boss I was sick and I went home early.

I went into my bedroom, grabbed my Bible and began to pray and read. I paced my room, holding the Bible against my chest and I began to speak to the spirit in me, "You can't stay," I said, "I don't want you, you have to leave." I read the promises of God aloud and continued to pray. I was scared—I didn't know what was happening to me. My body felt weird.

## Adam

I was working in the bush high up on a hill in the slasher when the Lord showed me to call Edith. *Ok,* I thought, *I'll call her after work.* The thought kept coming back, so insistent, I knew I had to call her right away. I got off the slasher, walked all the way up the hill where my truck was parked and called Edith on my cell phone.

## Edie

I jumped when my phone rang on the bedside table beside me.
"Hello?"
"Hi, Edith, what's going on?"
I can't explain the relief I felt when I heard Adam's voice on the other end of the line.
"Oh, Adam, I'm scared! Something's happening to me. I came home from work and I feel so strange."
"I'll be over as soon as I can." He said, "Remember you have authority in Christ. Stand strong in the Lord and in the power of *His* might."
"Ok."
I hung up the phone and continued to walk and talk to the Lord, not knowing—but just believing—that God was real and He was going to get me through this. I thanked Him for what He had done for me. I told Him I knew He could set me free, and I rebuked that spirit inside of me and told it to leave in Jesus' name.

Then I sat on the bed. I felt exhausted, but as I sat there God began to show me people in my life that I had wronged. I got out my notebook and began to write down names, people I needed to ask forgiveness of. I felt I was being cleansed in a deeper way. The Spirit of God was working in me strongly.

After I had written the list a new sensation came over me. It was like a pair of hands was squeezing a ball that was in me completely flat. I can't explain it well. It was a spiritual thing, but I knew God was squeezing something out and I was being healed of something that could've killed me. I have no proof, only a profound feeling, a *knowing* that that is what happened.

God was there all afternoon with me in my room.

When Adam came over that evening he invited a few people from our church group to come and pray for me. We went to the church basement, and I sat on a chair and they circled around me, six or seven people, to pray for me. Adam anointed my head with oil, and as he did I could *taste* it in my mouth, like a sweet perfume entering me, and I knew the work was done. So much had happened that day and I knew I was healed and that spirit in me was gone.

It's a strange feeling, to be delivered from a spirit. This had been with me since my youth, and when it was gone I felt very raw, nervous, and void. I remember looking around for Adam when the people were praying for me, because I felt so strangely alone.

"A spirit lives in your flesh," Adam explained to me later. "When it leaves, your flesh will notice the difference. Something's gone now. You need to fill that emptiness now with God. Focus on Him, and dwell on Him, and that spirit will never come back."

Still, over the next few weeks I found myself nervous. Every so often I would check myself, to see if the spirit might be back—but it never was!

In the next few months that followed my conversion, my life changed dramatically. I could sleep now. I had peace. The old Edie died that day the Lord touched me. My life became more abundant. I had had all those burdens: paying alimony and being alone. Now my divorce was finalized and Pam came to live with me. The Lord had blessed me. My business I had started less than six months earlier selling blinds began to flourish. I did it evenings and weekends and continued to work for Spruce Products on weekdays. It really helped me financially and I enjoyed the work.

I had never been baptized as a youth and when my other friends were being baptized I knew I couldn't. If I was going to be baptized it would be for something real in my life. Well, now something real had happened and I wanted to be baptized.

I went to the church I grew up in, mostly to please my mom, who wanted me to come to church now that I told her what the Lord had done for me. I signed up for the classes required for baptism and at the end of the course I gave my testimony to the church. The Spirit of God was there with me and I knew my testimony had touched people. There wasn't a dry eye in the building—so I was shocked when the pastor came up to me after the service and told me I wouldn't be able to be baptized.

"You have to agree to be a member of our church," he said stoically, "and you have refused to sign the membership papers."

It's true—I was through with religion and didn't want to be a member of any church, I belonged to God already, but was that any reason not to baptize me? I had just given a clear witness that God had made Himself real to me and I wanted to be baptized, but the church leaders remained staunch in their decision. I could not be baptized if I was not a member.

## Adam

Edith's testimony was powerful when she spoke at the church that Sunday.

When the church told her she couldn't be baptized, I offered to do it for her. I knew that any true believer could baptize another, and it seemed fitting that I baptize Edith anyway.

It was a beautiful fall morning in September when we drove to the lake. Edith knew someone with a cabin and we went there to have the beach access. I stood out by the shore as I waited for her to change.

The air was chilly, but the sun was bright and warm on my shoulders. I felt excited as I was standing there looking out at the water and praising God. What great things He had done in Edith's life, and a baptism always made me reflect on the things God had done in *my* life as well. I felt so honoured to have been part of God's plan for Edith. I was blessed to be able to baptize her.

She joined me by the shore dressed in her white baptismal gown—she was glowing from head to foot. I took her by the hand and together we walked out into the water. It was cold! But I felt warm inside, like the cold couldn't really penetrate the warmth coming from my inner man. Edith must have felt the same because she walked right beside me deep into the water and she never even shivered.

To explain a moment like this is hard. It's a spiritual thing to be baptized.

"Oh Father," Edith prayed as I held her there in the water, "thank you for what you've done in my life! For the change you've done in me—how you've made yourself real to me. I praise you, Lord, for all you've done. Don't stop. Continue this good work."

"Edith," I said after she had finished, "you have given your testimony before the people, and I have seen firsthand how God has touched your life. In accordance to the Word of God, I baptize you Edith in the name of the Father, and the Son Jesus Christ, and the Holy Spirit. And now as I baptize you, you are being buried with Christ in baptism." I immersed her completely in the water and lifted her back out and the Lord was glorified in it.

Two years later we were married. It was an outdoor wedding in Edie's backyard and all our children were there—and they were all part of the wedding party! Everyone was happy for us and it was a wonderful day. I couldn't help but marvel at the woman God had prepared for me. I knew I had asked God to give me someone who loved the Lord, but never had I imagined how blessed I would be to find one! The love Edith had towards her heavenly Father was something to behold. I would come to her place sometimes and hear her praying and worshipping God. That's how I knew I loved her.

Seeing how devoted she was to God, how she would read her Bible and pray and none of it was to get my attention—she didn't need me anymore—she had found her God, and now that she had Him she was a changed person and I loved her for it. I knew that's how a relationship should be—both people putting God first and then each other—and Edith was the first to agree.

Here was a lady at last who could work beside me serving the Lord and I knew God had great things in store for us.

## CHAPTER FIFTY-ONE

# GROUND TO DUST

I was working in the bush one day not long after Edith and I were married. When I worked with machinery I had a lot of time to think. I knew how to operate the slasher so well now it had become second nature. My hands would be working the levers to pick up and stack the logs and my mind would be thinking about the things of God. I had been thinking a lot lately about my calling from God. I knew God had called me to be a prophet, yet I wasn't satisfied with what I was doing, with where I was at in the Lord. Something was stopping me from going further. I knew the Lord had more work to do in my life.

"God," I spoke out loud, "I'm not happy where I am at in you. I want more. I want what the early church had—I want my life to be totally surrendered to you. No matter what the price." God was my ultimate priority. If I didn't have him, what was the point of all I had been through? I knew I would pursue God no matter what it cost me, yet I felt a twinge of fear as I said those words. God hears that kind of talk, sincere and from the heart. I knew that serving God came with a cost and that I would be tested. If I wanted God to work in my life I would have to give up control and let God break my character.

"Whatever you want to put me through, I will accept it." I said the words, but I had no idea of their consequences. Jesus said, 'Are you willing to drink of the cup I drink of, and be baptized with the baptism I will be baptized with?'

When Jesus was being prepared for his ministry the Bible says he was lead by the Spirit into the wilderness to be tempted of the devil. Most people think that Jesus only endured the three temptations that are mentioned at the end of the forty days, but I believe the devil was all over him during that time, and that he was tempted of many things. I didn't go through something that Jesus didn't go through also. How do you know you're getting closer to God? You get pressure from Satan like you've never had before.

The first thing I noticed was I began to feel anxiety. I'm usually very decisive and firm about what I want and feel—but suddenly I felt anxiety surrounding me. I thought I might be losing my mind. There was a fog around me that seemed to be stopping me from remembering things. I began to get scared. Was I going crazy?

I tried to quote scripture, something that always brought peace to my soul, but I couldn't remember any of the verses! They used to roll off my tongue and I could quote the Bible for hours, but suddenly I couldn't remember the verses or where they were found. "What's happening to me?" I lay on the couch and gripped my head, the anxiety hovering around me like a shroud. Satan was all over me.

"God, don't let me lose my mind!" I begged. Boy, if someone would have seen me then they would have carted me off to a mental institute. I could feel Satan on me, pressing me and I actually thought he might have the power to take my mind from me and leave me broken. Satan brought to mind the prayer I had prayed. *'Denounce god and I will leave you,'* he said.

I gasped, trying desperately to think, to find some solid ground in my mind to stand on. I actually thought about it. I considered how easy it would be to simply walk away from this, but God was real to me. He had done so much for me, I knew I could never turn away from that. His power in my life was far greater than anything the devil could throw at me.

"No," I said aloud, "I will not denounce God."

The pressure left and I was fine for a day or two and then Satan would come back. Each time was harder than the time before. I would walk for hours and just weep. I lost a lot of weight. I couldn't go to church or visit people. I was trapped in this wilderness. I was fighting a spiritual battle that was as real as anything I had ever experienced before. When people would come over to our house they would tell Edith they could see the glory of the Lord on me.

Edith was worried for me. She had just had her own spiritual experience with deliverance, but this was new to her and she didn't understand, "If you are a child of God," she said, "why is He allowing this to happen?"

"It's *because* I am a child of God," I told her. "I have to go through this."

That night I went to bed exhausted. Edith had worked a long day too and had fallen asleep. Suddenly I felt Satan come into the bedroom.

"Edith," I said, nudging her. "Wake up Edie, Satan is here attacking me. Can you pray for me?"

Edith crawled out of bed and went to get the oil.

The oppression on me was so strong.

Edie came back into the room and knelt down in front of me. She dipped oil onto her hands and placed them on me. I felt something in me wanting to fight her and I knew there was a spirit in me, because I didn't want to fight her, the spirit in me did. It knew it was going to have to leave. God had sent me to cast the spirits out of Edie and now he was using her to cast the spirits out of me!

When she was praying her voice sounded muffled to me. I couldn't focus on what she was saying but she talked to God. I had total faith her prayer would be answered. The prayer of a new baby in the Lord is so innocent and full of faith, it can move mountains. I felt that spirit come out of me and the relief was so great I fell back onto the bed, soaking wet and exhausted. I fell into a deep sleep finally at peace.

Three days later he was back.

"Edie," I tried to wake her up again. "He's back. Wake up, Edie."

"I'm too tired," She mumbled and went back to sleep.

I got up and I rebuked that devil. "Satan I command you by the Spirit of God, by the written Word, by the faith of Jesus Christ, and by the blood of Jesus, and in Jesus' name: get out and don't return."

Ok he left.

It was finished.

I laid back on the bed and I saw a cloud come over me. It was full of light, and it shimmered and moved over me. It was so beautiful. The presence of God was overshadowing me. The Lord showed me then in His Word, Matthew 21:44, that if you fall on a stone you will be broken, but if the stone falls on you, you will be ground to a powder. I was finished, completely ground down, there was nothing left of me.

I watched the cloud hover over me, and felt that glorious presence surround me until at last I cried, "God, let that cloud come into me!" The cloud seemed to burst, and the tiny pieces of mist settled into me.

The Word of the Lord came to me, *You will never be the same again. I will be with you, and everywhere you go I will walk before you and people will know that I walk with you.*

I was a different man coming out of the wilderness. God had to break my character and once He had broken my character I was tame. I had entered it a bronco, bucking and wild, and I had come out meek and mild, ready to do the will of God. He called me, He put me to the test, He broke me and He made me ready to be His servant.

CHAPTER FIFTY-TWO

# THE GIFT OF DISCERNMENT

One of the things Edith and I encountered often as we witnessed to people was evil spirits. People say that Christians have no evil spirits, but Jesus went to the synagogue to cast out devils and it's the same today. The devil is in church, and he does his best work keeping people comfortable, lulled into security, thinking they are safe and saved when they are really nowhere with God.

One time I was in a new church with Edith. We didn't know anybody there. A man was up at the front speaking, telling people how much the Lord loves them, but I could see he had spirits in him!

It wasn't my church and there wasn't much I could do, but after the service I was talking to a woman. Edith was beside me when suddenly with my spiritual eyes I saw the man looking at me. I was carrying on a conversation with the woman but at the same time I was totally aware that this man was walking around behind me, starring at me.

Edith saw the man and she said it was like he was looking right through me.

The spirit in *him* recognized the spirit of God in *me*.

Suddenly he stood right in front of me and looked at me. I could see the spirit in him starring right at me. I looked right at him and said, "Who are you?"

He jumped back and said, "I'm a Christian!" and he hurried off into the crowd.

On the way home Edith and I talked about it. She was excited to have seen something so spiritual. I wondered though, why hadn't I cast the devil out of him?

The Lord showed me he didn't want to be set free.

I phoned the pastor up that night and asked if we could meet sometime. The Lord had shown me something in his church I needed to tell him about. The pastor wanted nothing to do with what I saw and he never called back to meet with me.

Another time the Spirit impressed on me to go to a revival meeting in Pelican Rapids. I didn't know what I was supposed to do there, just that I needed to go. That's usually the way God works and it's always exciting.

Edie and I went to Pelican Rapids and got there just as the service was starting. The music was loud and showy, but I liked the message and the speaker seemed very genuine. The meeting went very late and it was a long drive home, so Edith and I had to leave before the service ended. I didn't get a chance to find out what I was supposed to do there. The next day I drove up alone, and went early so I could catch the speaker before the service started.

I stood at the door of the church waiting for the pastor to arrive.

"Excuse me," I said as the evangelist and his wife approached. "My name is Adam, I live in Swan River, I was hoping you would stop by for a visit on your way back to Oklahoma City—I know it's on the way—my wife and I would love to have you."

I gave him a paper with my address and phone number.

"Well, sure," the speaker said as he shook my hand. "We might just do that."

A few days later when the revival meetings were over I got a phone call saying they would be stopping by as planned.

When he and his wife arrived, I still didn't know what God had wanted me to do! We were sitting outside and it started getting cold, so Edie invited them in. We moved inside and sat down across from each other in the living room. Edie and I on one couch and the pastor and his wife on the other.

Suddenly I fastened my eyes on the woman and said to her, "You have spirits and God is going to set you free."

Her face became twisted and fearful. "I'm so afraid!" she said. The spirit was manifesting in her face and speaking.

"You're not afraid," I said to the woman. "The spirit *in* you is afraid".

"I'm scared!" she started to cry.

"You're not scared," I said. "The devil has been lying to you-- you're not afraid."

I put my hands on her and rebuked the devil.

She opened her eyes and looked at me. The fear in her was gone.

"You're not afraid," I repeated. "It was the spirit in you that was scared. See?"

She began to cry as she told me she had had this spirit with her since she was a little girl and she didn't think she would ever be free of it.

She was like the woman in the gospel of Luke who had been bound by the spirit of infirmity for eighteen years. Now she was set free and she glorified God. Even the Evangelist was overwhelmed with what God had done that day.

His timing is so perfect.

When we are obedient to God, he puts people into our life who need help so that he can use us to help them and you need discernment from God for that. Before God uses you to perform a miracle you first need to have discernment to know *who* to pray for and *what* to pray for. So often people pray without being in the will of God, and the prayer goes unanswered. It is not up to me who I pray for—it is God who shows me who He wants me to speak to, and Him who gives me the words to speak. You can't make things happen in the flesh. It is God, or nothing.

CHAPTER FIFTY-THREE

# MINISTERING

A minister and I were heading to a meeting up North one night, but before we went, there were a few people the minister wanted to talk to.

We pulled up in front of a house.

"I'll just be a minute," the minister said. He went into the house while I waited in the car. I could see through the shadows in the window that he was talking to a lady in the house. It didn't take long before he was walking back to the car, but instead of coming to the driver's side, he opened my door.

"Come inside," he said. "I need you to talk to her."

I didn't know what to say but I followed him back into the house.

The minister spoke to her in her native language and he must have explained who I was. She nodded and looked over at me as I sat down at the table in front of her. Nobody talked for a couple of minutes, there was complete silence. All of a sudden the Lord began to show me things about her.

I leaned forward and looked right into her eyes. "You want to kill yourself," I said. "In fact, four days ago you tried to kill yourself and it didn't work."

I saw the flash in her eyes of recognition, remorse, and deep sadness.

"That's a spirit," I explained. "I'm going to pray for you at the meeting tonight, and you're going to be delivered."

I could see something happening as I spoke to her. She was drinking my words hungrily. She was believing. There was a light of hope in her eyes.

That night at the meeting I preached and held an altar call at the end of the service. That lady was one of the people that came forward. I anointed her with oil and prayed over her, casting out the spirit of suicide and speaking life into her. As I prayed she began to cry, and it was as if the glory of the Lord was upon her. Her face shone. She began to speak her native tongue, and someone came over to interpret.

"She says, 'When you walked into my house today I felt the presence of the Lord. And it has been with me ever since.' She says, 'I have been totally set free.'" The man interpreted.

The lady seemed to be shining from head to toe—that's what freedom looks like after being oppressed by the devil! There's such a visible change in a person after they have been set free from bondage and experience the freedom of Christ.

CHAPTER FIFTY-FOUR

## SHARING EXCITEMENT

Edie and I knew we wouldn't live in Swan River long term. We had bought some apartment buildings in Steinbach and already I was travelling back and forth there making plans to build a second apartment block. I would go to Steinbach during the week while Edie worked in Swan River, and then I'd go back to be with her on the weekends, or she would come out to Steinbach to be with me.

We had plans to move permanently to Steinbach once Edie retired.

During those days alone in Steinbach I would run into people.

Usually when people first meet me they find me funny. I like to entertain and tell stories and it's natural for me to command a crowd. I find that because of this first impression I get invited to a lot of social events, which usually involve the church. Then, when I get my foot in the door and start talking about the Lord, people seem surprised. I don't come off as a religious person because I'm not, so it's surprising when you hear a big loud man like me talking about the Lord.

Edie and I were at a church fundraiser one evening. I'll always remember that event, because a woman had been prayed for to be healed of cancer. She had stood up to give a testimony of her healing, and as she spoke I looked over at Edie and said, 'That woman isn't healed.' I don't know why God shows me the things he does, but I could see clearly through the eyes of my inner man that she was not healed, and was still very sick. It made me sad to think that people had prayed for her of their own will and told her she had been healed. We are not the ones who decide who is healed and who is not. I can never pray for someone who God has not shown me to pray for, and expect a miracle. It is God who heals, not man, and without God we can do nothing. We found out that she died a few months later.

It was also at that meeting where I met a man who later invited me to a prayer meeting. He had thought I was funny and just wanted to have a good time at the prayer meeting with me. He didn't know me at all and I knew he had no idea that God was such a real presence in my life.

To be honest, I didn't really want to go to the prayer meeting. When I pray I like to be alone. On top of that, the meeting was scheduled for seven in the morning and it was the dead of winter. I owned a diesel and that was reason enough not to go.

I went to bed that night already having decided I wouldn't go to the prayer meeting, but sure enough, I was awoken during the night and felt the Spirit impressing me to go. "I don't even remember where it is," I mumbled to God in my tired state. *Uncle Jakes*, the name of the restaurant came to me right away. I glanced at my alarm clock. I had just enough time to start my truck and let it warm up while I got ready. I sighed, tossed back the covers and rolled out of bed. "This better be good," I told the Lord. I trudged outside in the bitter cold to start the truck.

When I got to the restaurant a waitress saw me looking around and offered help.

"I'm looking for the men's prayer meeting." I peered around the restaurant looking for the man who had invited me. I didn't mean to be loud but I'm sure everyone heard me. Someone waved me over and I joined a group of men and sat down at the end of the table. I didn't talk to anyone and nobody talked to me, but I'm sure everybody was thinking, *'who is this guy and what is he doing here?'*

I sat through the short program waiting for the Spirit to prompt me. He had told me to come and here I was—and I knew something was going to happen.

We began to eat our breakfast when the man sitting beside me asked, "So, where are you from?"

That was it! I opened my mouth and the words began to pour out of me.

I began to speak about how our lives change when we encounter God. There was compassion inside me, I felt the Spirit yearning to draw these people to Him. I told them about the woman at the well. I pointed out how the disciples had gone out and brought back food from the town, but when the woman went to town she brought the whole town back with her! The difference in her after she encountered Jesus. She said, "Come and meet the man who told me everything I ever did!" Now, that's powerful! She was a changed person, and when we encounter God we change too. His impact in our lives will show. As I spoke I felt excited inside, there were prominent people at this meeting, and I felt so thankful that God had had mercy on me and chosen to touch me and use me. I didn't deserve His grace, but I was sure thankful for it!

"How long have you been a Christian?" one man asked me.

"Since I was twenty," I said.

"Shame on us," he looked at the people and said, "we have been Christians our whole lives and we are not excited like this man."

## CHAPTER FIFTY-FIVE

## A PASTOR IS CHOSEN

I ran into a man at a coffee shop one day and somehow we started talking about the Lord. He was French like me and we got along well and before I knew it he was inviting me to speak at his church. He was an elder there. They currently didn't have a pastor so they had been having guest speakers every so often until a new pastor was hired.

I agreed to speak. I'm not sure I've ever turned down an opportunity to preach!

I had no idea what I was in for.

Edie and I went that next Sunday and I gave a simple sermon, just sharing some of my testimony and what God had done for me. The church liked what they heard. They were in the middle of a split; their pastor had left and no one could agree on what to do next. Controversy was everywhere. I preached several more sermons and did some Bible studies over the course of the next few weeks. Some people liked what I had to say and wanted me to apply, others called me a false prophet and didn't want anything to do with me (or my wife). Arguments would erupt, people would stand up and voice their opinions freely. Anger, discontentment and strife were everywhere.

After one particular argument I noticed an ex-Hutterite couple in the back of the church getting up to leave.

"Don't walk out," I pleaded.

I saw the lady pause, her hand already on the door.

"I know it's terrible," I said. "There's lots of wrong stuff going on—but don't leave yet. God's going to do something in your life," I said. I knew it was true. "Give me a chance."

They stayed. I later found out their names were Kenny and Melva, and they would become dear friends of mine in the future.

I hadn't been looking to be a pastor. I'd always been more of an evangelist on the go, but these people needed help. I agreed to be interviewed for a pastoral position.

Several people arrived for the interview. We sat there waiting to be inspected by the church board. Each candidate got up to speak about what responsibilities they were willing to carry, what they would bring to the church body, and what they expected their wages to be. When it came to my turn I was nearly ready to leave the meeting. "Listen," I said to them. "You can't hire me, plain and simple."

I could see the shocked looks on the board's faces as I said the words. Why would I agree to the interview and then refuse the job?

"I don't work for man," I said, "and I don't work for money. If you were to pay me, I'd have to preach what you tell me to—and me, I don't preach anything unless God tells me to—I learned that a long time ago."

I looked around the room. "Secondly," I added, "Jesus said freely you have received, freely give! Why would I charge you for the good news of the kingdom of God? I'll be your pastor if you want me to be—but I'm telling you now you won't all like it."

I would be their pastor if that's what they wanted. I certainly knew I could help them. But I would minister as I was led by God, not under the direction of man—and I knew that would be a problem for some.

There were others who wanted to hold my past against me. "He's been divorced," they said, whispering together. "Is that the kind of leader we want for our church?" "And he calls his wife a minister. How can a woman be a leader in a church? It's not Biblical" "But this man has so much wisdom! He knows the scriptures! I've felt the anointing of God in his messages."

I sat back, having said my piece, and waited. The arguing grew louder until finally one of the elders, Denis (the one I had first met at the coffee shop), stood up and said, "Adam will be our pastor, and that is final."

I became the pastor and half the church left.

CHAPTER FIFTY-SIX

## MEETING ED

Ed I saw him before he saw me, but I still looked up and feigned surprise as he came towards me and spoke.

"Good morning." His voice was loud and boisterous.

"Morning," I nodded.

"What do you have there?" The man tipped his head and indicated the Bible I was carrying.

"... It's my Bible."

"Oh," his eyes smiled at me, but I could sense he was searching for something. "Know anything about it?"

I laughed before I could stop myself. "I sure hope so," I said. I'd been teaching Sunday school for years now and was on about every board and directory the church had to offer.

"I'm Adam. I'm your new landlord." He shook my hand and waited for me to give him my name.

"Ed," I said.

He smiled at me, "Well, Ed, it's good for you to meet me." He said it as a joke and I laughed uncomfortably, but I wasn't sure that it *was* good for me to meet him.

I saw him there in his coveralls about to mow the lawn. I knew he did it on Sundays because I'd seen him do it before. He didn't go to church much, and he clearly wasn't from around here—his accent seemed French maybe. I'd have thought he was just a labourer if he hadn't told me just now that he owned these apartment blocks. Maybe I was supposed to witness to him.

I was at my brother's apartment the next time I encountered Adam. My brother and I were sitting in the living room chatting together when I heard a loud voice coming down the hall. We knew he was at the door before he knocked.

"Come in," my brother said.

Adam pushed open the door. He was wearing his coveralls again and looked to be in the middle of a task, "Yes, hi—I don't want to interrupt you I've just got a quick question," he said. "Has your hot water tank been leaking at all?"

"Not that I know of," my brother said.

"Okay." Adam had his hand on the door to leave, but then he turned to us and said, "You know, God is so good. I was in the mud up to my knees at the University of Manitoba when the Word of the Lord came to me 'you're going to work hard, die, then what?'—and it changed my life."

Adam continued to talk, just briefly, and my eyes were glued to him. The way he spoke, so earnest and open and sure that what he said was true—I hadn't seen that type of confidence before. God spoke to *him*? I tried to think back to a time where God had spoken to me and I couldn't recall a single one. I was a minister in the church, a Sunday school teacher, chairman of the board of directors for a Bible camp. People looked to me for spiritual guidance and direction. Yet God had never spoken to me. But this man spoke about God like he knew him personally.

He was out the door before I had a chance to gather my thoughts, but already something had begun to work in me. It was the first time I saw that maybe I didn't have what I thought I did. Maybe all this work I was doing was just that—work—and it had nothing to do with whether or not I knew God at all.

## CHAPTER FIFTY-SEVEN

## OPENING THE WORD

After meeting Ed at the apartments I began to put in more of an effort to get to know him. I had seen the few times I'd talked that he really listened to me. He was attentive and he was being drawn. I knew he worked in construction as I'd seen his trailer parked alongside the apartments, so I asked him one day if he'd help me repair the fences.

Ed needed help, but not the kind of help he thought he did. He was stressed about his finances and he wanted me to help by investing in his new company. I knew I would help him. God had given me wisdom in business, but the timing was not right. He needed to hit rock bottom and, when he was ready, then I would help him—and we'd do it my way—not his. I never told him that of course but I did suggest we do a Bible study together sometime.

It took about two years before Ed was willing to talk. I knew he was in a dark place. I could see it in his face. He worked so hard for his church. He was stressed about money, had three young children and struggled to make ends meet. I had been there before and I knew what it was like to feel like you were constantly struggling just to keep above the surface. He needed a touch from the living God, and I knew I could help him!

Finally, I called him up one day and asked if I could do a Bible study with him and his wife.

"Sure," he said, his voice monotone and bored. I knew he was done with Bible studies. He probably had them all the time, but this one would be different. I was sure.

I drove up to their house (they had moved out of the apartments) and knocked on their door at nine o'clock sharp on Tuesday evening.

Ed answered the door and gave me a confused look. He always seemed surprised by me, like I wasn't what he expected. Well, I couldn't blame him. I was wearing sweats and a comfy shirt, and I was here to teach—not to make a good impression.

"Come in," he said. "Would you like coffee?"

"No thanks," I said.

I walked into their living room and looked around. I pulled the coffee table out of the way and dragged an easy chair close to the couch. I wanted to be able to see them both clearly and be close to them. "Do you have your Bibles?"

"Yes," Ed said, still looking slightly uncomfortable.

"Good, bring them here." I motioned for them to sit on the couch across from me. I hadn't brought my Bible along, but I already knew the passage I would be teaching them tonight. There was an excitement in me—I knew God was moving.

"Let's pray," I began.

## Ed

When Adam showed up at our house that first night for Bible study I didn't know what to think. He came to our door wearing sweatpants, walked in without a Bible, and started moving the furniture around!

"Open your Bibles to Matthew 5," he said.

I did as he asked, and so did my wife, Jules. We were sitting on the couch together and he sat directly in front of us.

"You've maybe read this a hundred times, but now let me tell you what it means," He said. And then Adam, that big rough man with a loud voice, dropped to his knees in front of us, and with a passion and authority I had never seen before he began to open the scriptures to us. He would quote verse by verse, sometimes word by word and then say, 'ok stop' and he would explain each part. I had never heard some of the stuff he was saying—but it was right there in front of me.

"Who is a man's right hand?" he asked, and he would make us really think about what Jesus was saying. "Who is a man's right eye?"

Adam knelt there before us for nearly two hours and his questions burned in me. I didn't want to accept what he was saying, but when he spoke it was like I could see everything in a new light. The word was beginning to have life as he opened it up to me.

When he got up to leave, he prayed for us.

"Can I come again next week?" he asked.

"Sure, ok," I mumbled. My mind was buzzing with everything I had just heard and experienced. I felt like telling him he was a false prophet and to never come back again. How could he be right and everybody else I knew be wrong? But at the same time he backed up everything he said with scripture. There was a deep hunger in me for more, and with the way things were going for me, I really didn't have anything to lose.

CHAPTER FIFTY-EIGHT

## GOD TOUCHES ED

**Adam**

I came to their house the next week at nine o clock again and did the same thing: moved the furniture, sat them down in front of me and went through the scriptures with them, verse by verse, showing them the things God had shown me when he had opened my understanding years ago. I spoke with authority because I had complete confidence in God. The verses were ingrained in me. I was so familiar with the Bible I often used it as a dictionary when I needed to know how to spell a word.

Nothing big happened at this Bible study but as I was leaving I asked if I could pray for them. "Sure," Ed said.

I don't remember my exact words, but Ed looked up at me as I finished the prayer. He thrust his finger at me and said, "What are you talking about: God has heard our cries?" he looked upset.

The answer came right out of me. "Three days ago I saw you cry out to the Lord. He has heard your cries and has sent me to help you."

A look of complete shock washed over him. He looked over at Jules. "What were you doing three days ago?" He asked her.

"We had that big fight," she admitted. "You left. I went into our room and cried out to God." She had tears in her eyes as she looked at me and then glanced away.

"Three days ago," Ed said, and he starred at me now with wonder, "I was at the end of my rope. I know I don't have God—he's never done anything for me!" There was hurt and frustration in his voice. "I've given so much to the church, and what do I have to show for it?" He shook his head. "...but three days ago I went down into the basement and begged God, if he really was real, to make himself real to me, and if he did—I would worship him."

## Ed

When Adam prayed that prayer I knew there was no way he could have known Jules and I had called out to God. I didn't even know that Jules had—yet his words were so specific: *'Thank you Lord that you heard **their** cries.'* Either Adam was what he said he was, a man of God sent by God to help us, or he was a phoney, and, if he was a phoney, was it just a shot in the dark that he prayed those words?

So I challenged him. "What do you mean 'he has heard our cries'?"

His answer changed everything. Three days ago. Adam couldn't have known that, not so specifically, this had to have been God. And that meant three things: God was real, God had heard my prayer, and God had sent Adam to help me.

I felt everything as if it were spinning around me. My mind was so busy figuring out all the implications of this. What did it all mean? What did I have to do now? How did I get God in my life?

I hungrily began to search the scriptures. I knew I didn't have God. I knew that God didn't speak to me. The spirit of God didn't stir in me. I didn't have power. Nothing spiritual had happened in my life up to this point, and yet the whole New Testament was full of promises from God! 'I will make my abode with you.' 'I will manifest myself to you.' 'I will teach you all things, yea the deep things of God.' It was all there in front of me, and I knew I didn't have it. They were promises from God to the believers...so why didn't I have them? Somewhere in all this I was missing something.

"Show me, God!" I cried out to the Lord. "Teach me and I will believe it! I need your Spirit. You promised it, and you've got to give it to me, and I'm not going to stop asking for it until I get it! Whatever it takes!" I was broken before God. I knew my life was nothing without Him.

It was like that for several weeks, me crying out to God for His Spirit, calling on the promises of God, searching the scriptures, praying, and waiting.

Then one night it happened. We were having Bible study in our living room again and Adam was speaking, when suddenly I heard the Lord say *through* Adam, "Come unto me, all you who labour and are heavy laden, and I will give you rest." Adam was kneeling with his arms spread wide. "Take my yoke upon you, and learn of me; for I am meek and lowly in heart: and ye shall find rest unto your souls. For my yoke is easy, and my burden is light."

It was Adam's mouth that moved and spoke, but the only way I can explain it is that God spoke directly to me through him. I felt the words wash over me, and it was as if everything in me just began to drain out. 'Come unto me all you who labour and are heavy laden.' All my works, everything I'd done for the church, I saw suddenly how heavy those burdens were upon me, and even as I saw them I felt them draining away. All my religious efforts to please people, trying so hard to be good and perfect, my tiredness of working for my salvation, all my trying to establish my own righteousness... everything was draining away, and I began to feel a glow in me. It filled me and warmed me and I knew it was my inner man! This was the Spirit of God. He had given it to me. I felt it come to life inside me with those words 'come unto me and rest...'

I sat back in my chair and just let the feeling wash over me. All my life I thought I'd had the Spirit of God because I'd said a prayer once—but in all that time I'd never experienced God. The Bible says what's supposed to happen, and now I was seeing that come to fruition in me. God had given me His Spirit, just like the Bible said he would. I could feel it now in me. It wasn't something I had to work for or look for. I had it because I believed. I had asked for it—and he's good! He *wants* us to have his Spirit.

I looked up and watched as Adam continued to speak. He certainly wasn't what I pictured a man of God to look like, yet God had used this man mightily in my life already, and my journey had only just begun.

CHAPTER FIFTY-NINE

# SHILOH

Over thirty years ago I had had a vision. I had been standing outside the property line of the farm where I grew up in St. Labre, and I had seen in its place a beautiful cabin surrounded by trees and gardens. People were walking in small groups together around the yard, they were excited to be there to see what God was going to do. I knew instinctively that this was a place of rest, and peace, and I wanted to call it 'Shiloh.'

After I had the vision I carved a crude sign out of wood with the name *Shiloh* on it, and left the sign on the property.

It passed through a couple hands over the years, but when the farm finally became available for purchase from one of my brothers, I snapped up the opportunity. I'd owned the property now for about ten years, and I felt it was time to start building.

It was cold out. I tucked my hands into my jacket and watched my breath puff out in tiny clouds that disappeared as quickly as they came. Already I could feel the tips of my ears stiff and red with cold. It reminded me of being a kid again, never dressed warm enough against the winter freeze. My brother Joseph stood beside me, he wasn't dressed any better than I was.

"Ready, Joseph?" I asked my brother, I spoke in French to him because he preferred that.

"Oui," he said, nodding and smiling.

I picked up a jerry can full of diesel and nodded my head towards the old house, "Let's go then!"

Just as we were heading to the house an old pickup truck drove into the yard. I paused and went to see what they wanted.

"Is this house for sale?" the couple in the truck wanted to know. "We'll offer you a good price."

I stood there contemplating. "Let me think about it for a minute," I said, "have a look around the yard if you like."

Joseph and I trudged over the frost tipped grass and pushed open the door of the old Adams' house. It creaked in protest and hung crookedly on its rusted hinges. It was really nothing but a shell now, but I still felt a rush of emotion fill my chest.

Should I sell the place for a profit? I was, after all, a businessman. Making easy money was what I loved to do. If I burnt down the house and built a retreat here it would cost me a lot of money. But if I sold the place I'd be giving up on my dream and my vision for Shiloh.

"Are you coming?" Joseph asked. He was already at the top of the stairs waiting for me.

"Relax," I said. "I'll be there in a minute."

I walked up the stairs, took one last look around, and then slowly and deliberately walked around the rooms, pouring the fuel carefully along the floor, dousing the wall now and then to make sure everything would burn. Joseph did the same on his side and then we met back at the stairs.

"You go on ahead," I said to Joseph. "Wait for me outside."

"Ok."

I listened for his boots to exit the house, then fumbled in my pockets for a match. I lit the match, dropped it, and watched the flames instantly flare to life. I jogged down the stairs quickly and joined my brother a safe distance away.

The couple that had wanted to buy the place looked at me in shock. "What are you *doing?*" The man asked, indignant.

"Trust me, you don't want this place!" I said to them, pointing over my shoulder at the house. "It's going up in flames as we speak!"

I had decided that seeing the vision of Shiloh come to fruition was more important than any profit I could make on this house. The couple drove off, insulted.

Smoke soon joined the clouds of our breath in the chilly air and heat waves began to glisten around the house. Bright hot tongues of fire leapt across the roof now, and black smoke began to pour out of the windows and front door. It didn't take long for the whole house to be engulfed in flame.

Night soon crept in around us and in the darkness the house glowed a dull orange, a smouldering heap of char and debris.

"I guess that's it," Joseph said. "That was about the biggest fire we've made, eh, Art?" he smiled proudly. "You should have seen the rats running."

"Yep, that was a pretty big fire." I took one last look at the smoking pile of ashes and envisioned the cabin that was going to take its place.

"Let's go," I said to Joseph. "It's cold out here!"

CHAPTER SIXTY

---

## DRIVING TRUCK

I liked driving truck. Ever since that first time I'd sat in a semi and told my boss I could drive it—well—I've never lost my passion for figuring things out. Back then I'd stared at all the levers and pedals and thought, what the heck was I going to do? Now it seemed like second nature. I turned the radio on and barrelled through Marion Street, veering into the right lane as I prepared to turn.

I had just made the turn when the truck started shaking violently. I heard a jarring, tearing sound and I felt the wheel jerk out of my hands. The truck lurched sideways—I had no control of the steering wheel. I slammed on the brakes, shifting and clutching trying to gain control of the truck. I managed to pull off to the side a bit, jumped out of the cab and bent under the front tires to inspect the damage. Sure enough, the tie rod had snapped and was dragging on the ground. Any other time I would have just called for a tow truck—but for some reason I just looked at the tie rod dangling there on the pavement and climbed back up into the cab.

When I talk about God doing miracles, I sometimes explain it to people saying, 'You have to lose your head.' Most of the things God does through us don't make sense. If we thought about it we'd definitely do it another way. So we have to lose our heads. We get out of our own mind, and into the mind of Christ. Well, that's what happened here.

I knew it made no sense to start that truck up and keep driving, yet that's exactly what I did—and as I did it, I knew God would take over. Like Peter jumping out of the boat to join Jesus on the water, I jumped into the truck and jammed the key into the ignition.

I drove half a mile with no steering. I slowed down and the truck turned right. It went right again at the next stop. I crossed Marion and turned left to get to the repair shop. A truck pulled beside me and I stopped, and in the truck was my foreman.

"How are you driving this thing?" He called to me. "The tie rod is broken."

"I'm not driving, God is."

He got out of his truck with a roll of duct tape. "I'll at least try and patch this up until you reach the shop." He got under the truck and wrapped the duct tape around the tie rods, securing them together.

I thanked him and kept driving. I shifted into gear, took my foot off the brake and merged back into traffic like nothing had happened. I would shift, but the truck would drive. I turned right on Panet Road. Hit Dugald and turned left, but by now the duct tape had fallen off and the tie rod was dragging again.

Four guys outside saw me when I finally pulled into the yard, the tie rod clearly dragging on the gravel beneath the truck. I shut off the truck and got out of the cab.

"How did you drive this thing?" The mechanic asked, staring at me like I was crazy. "The tie rod is completely gone."

I felt a little shaky now that it was over, but I was excited too. This was a miracle! "I wasn't driving—God was!"

They laughed nervously—they all knew I was a pastor so they didn't want to mock me—but I'm sure they were all trying to think of some other way this could have happened.

The mechanic climbed up into the cab and started the truck up to drive it into the garage. If I had driven it, he figured he could drive it too. The truck started and immediately the tires swivelled different directions.

One man whistled. "You're one lucky man," he said, looking at me sideways. "There could have been an accident, the tie rod breaking like that."

"I know." I said. "I'm telling you, God drove the truck! I shifted and changed gears, but he held the steering wheel!" It was an incredible experience that nobody could deny.

I liked to drive truck, but I guess God liked to drive truck too.

CHAPTER SIXTY-ONE

# THE MESSAGES FLOW

When I was ordained pastor of the church many people left, but I was not concerned. It was not my job to choose who would hear the messages God had prepared in me—but just to speak them. I might be a pastor now, but I refused to let that title change who I was as a person. I just wanted to help people, (and pastors too).

We ended up leaving the big church building and renting a small clinic in Lorette. Every Sunday I would go up to the front to speak, often not knowing what I would speak about, and every Sunday God would come through for me. I would have a message for the people every time. I didn't need days to prepare because God had prepared me years ago—those days I had spent on my back because of that neck injury—pouring through the scriptures and being led verse by verse as if God was standing right over my shoulder pointing them out to me. Those messages now were coming into my remembrance and I didn't need notes. It was as if they were right there in front of me. I'd speak and the Lord would show me where to go next.

Some mornings I would wake up at four just to be with God. I loved being alone with him, and sometimes the early hours were the only time to get those opportunities. God was more than just a Father to me. He was my friend. Through all these years He had never abandoned me. He worked with me—corrected me—taught me, but most importantly, He loved me. These early mornings He would come to me, and we would talk together, and I would just dwell in His presence, in this secret place He had for me.

Worship would be on my heart. My love for my Father resonated in me. I'd begin to read scripture and the presence of God would instantly be there. I'd go from verse to verse, passage to passage, amazed at what was emerging each time. Always there would be a message. I never left my time with God feeling empty. Some days I would arrive at church not knowing what I would speak and then just at the right time the Lord would reveal it to me! He never let me down.

What a blessing I would receive each Sunday. I got to feed the people God had brought to me and, as I fed them, I myself would be fed! God was a real, steady force in my life, and many miracles were happening in the lives of the people who were coming to listen to the messages. I always wanted to be available for those people and available for God to use me!

CHAPTER SIXTY-TWO

## GOD WORKS IN THE LIVES OF HIS PEOPLE

One person whose life changed was Becky. She and her husband were at a rough point in their relationship and I had been giving them council.

I was in Winnipeg one day when I felt the Lord tell me to go talk to Becky. I changed directions I was driving and went to the clinic. It wasn't her day to work but the Lord had shown me she would be there.

I walked into the small clinic and went right to the receptionist. "Where's Becky?" I asked. "I need to speak to her."

Becky had heard me from the back room where she was sitting. She had been crying, but she came out to see me. "How did you know I was here?" She asked. "I didn't tell anybody I would be here today."

"The Lord showed me where you were," I said. "And he sent me here to help you."

We talked and I was able to share with her the message God had given me.

One day the Word of the Lord came to me: *Call Becky*. I called her up and asked if I could speak to her. She immediately became defensive. "If it's about my husband and I, I don't want to hear it." She said, and she hung up.

A moment later I again felt the need to call her.

"Come over," I said to Becky. "I have something to tell you. I want to talk about *you*."

She came.

I was working in the front yard with Ed when I saw her walk around the house to see me. I immediately put down my tools. "Come inside," I said, leading her into the cool air-conditioning of my house. We went into the living room and I offered her a chair. I was waiting to see what the Lord had for me to say to her and, if he didn't speak soon, I had a thing or two to tell her myself!

I sat down across from her and met her eyes. Immediately I felt the overwhelming love of God towards her. She burst into tears right there in front of me.

"Come here. I'm going to pray for you," I said.

I placed my hand on her and felt the Lord. "Oh Father," I prayed, "set her free from this bondage." I don't remember the words I prayed, but Becky looked up at me after. A huge smile lit her face. She looked bright, and light, and free!

"Thank you Pastor Adam," She said.

Salvation had come to Becky this day. A great work had been done in the Spirit. "You feel set free today," I said. "But you don't fully know the impact of what this prayer has done for you. God has touched you today."

I went back outside to finish my work and Becky went home.

I saw Becky two weeks later and the glow in her was so noticeable. Her whole countenance had changed. A miracle had taken place in her life. She had been set free from bondage during that prayer, and I later found out she had been healed as well.

CHAPTER SIXTY-THREE

# THE QUESTIONS

I was invited to a barbeque after church one Sunday by Kenny and Melva. They had friends that they wanted me to meet, and I was excited to talk to them more about the Lord outside the walls of the church building. It was at this barbecue that I met a couple. They had just recently left the Hutterite colony and were searching for a church that had a real living excitement about the Lord, something that had been lacking in the church they had left.

When the man sat down beside me at the barbecue I could see he was hungrily listening to what I was saying about God. He began asking me questions and, the more I talked, the more excited he got.

Early one Sunday morning I was at my office at church when that couple came in to see me. They had moved into a new house when they left the colony, and ever since then there had been trouble in the house. Their children were scared at night and not sleeping. Could I help?

"Your house has spirits," I said to him. "Don't worry about it. I'm going to pray for you this morning and then I'll come over to your house and cast them out."

When they came forward for prayer after the service that morning I saw a black cloud lift up out of them as they walked down the aisle. There had been a spirit in them and it knew it had to leave, even before I said the prayer. The authority we have in Jesus is just amazing! We don't even have to do or say anything sometimes for the work to be done. Just believe.

I drove over to their house that evening and I anointed it with oil, cast out the spirits in the name of Jesus, and dedicated this house to God. They have never had problems with that house since.

They were still hungry for more of God and God began to work in their lives. The man was set free from anxiety and the woman went from wearing head coverings and long dresses to being free under the covering of grace. Never once had I told her to stop covering her head, but I preached to her the Holy Spirit is our covering and that our righteousness comes from God.

The man called me after one Bible study and told me something he was struggling with. "I always feel so good at the Bible study," he confessed. "I am learning and the Word is being opened to me, but whenever it's over and we go home, I am overwhelmed by doubt and depression. I feel completely empty."

"That's the Devil," I told him. "He want's to rob you of what you receive. Get a piece of paper." I waited for him to comply.

"Ok," he said, "What else?"

"Write down what I tell you. Is your wife leaving you? Are your children sick? Did you lose your job?"

I waited for him to write the questions down.

"Well?" I asked.

"Of course not. Everything is fine."

"Then you have no reason to be depressed and that's just Satan trying to bring you down. Rebuke him and he will flee. And the next time you feel that way, take out the sheet of paper and tell Satan where to go. But I'll tell you right now—he hears me speak and he's already gone. He won't be back."

Those feelings never did come back.

CHAPTER SIXTY-FOUR

## VISITING THE COLONY

I had been ministering to several ex-Hutterite families lately, and had even done some Bible studies with their relatives that were still living on the colony. The meeting were always done outside the colony and always in secret, but one day I was invited to come to the colony to visit a family there. I was taken in undercover because if the elders had known I was there to do a Bible study they would *not* have been happy. I had never been to a Hutterite colony before, and I found the way they lived fascinating. Everything was so organized. There was a place and a schedule for every person and every job.

I was sitting in the living room shortly after I had arrived when a knock sounded on the door.

"*Shh!*" The couple I was witnessing to cautioned me to be quiet. "They're coming to check up on us."

I waited for the man to go away.

"Did anyone else know I was here today?" I asked them.

"No, we didn't tell anyone."

After talking some more with the family, they began to give me a tour of the colony. They showed me the kitchens, and the pantry, where all the canning was kept. Walls and walls of beautifully canned preserves. They showed me where they ate, the men on one side and the women on the other. There was a room where the shoes were made, where the sewing was done, a room for every job and task. I'd never seen such an organized operation before! When we got outside they took me to see the machinery and the barns. We walked past the gardens, ripe with produce. At last we were on our way back to their house when we walked past one room where the computers were kept. As soon as I walked into the room I saw something spiritual.

"This place is bugged." I said.

The couple looked at me strangely. "What do you mean?"

"From this room, people can know what's going on in everybody's homes on the colony." There was no proof of what I said. I just knew. The Lord had shown it to me.

I left after that and went back to Steinbach, but a few months later that couple told me that it had been discovered that the elder's had indeed had the colony under audio surveillance. They had been monitoring the lives of the people inside their homes through the recording equipment in that room where we had been standing.

CHAPTER SIXTY-FIVE

## BASEBALL

Ed's wife, Jules, was also being touched by the Bible studies, we had been having together. She was receiving life and freedom from the Word of God and it was such a relief after the bondage of religion that she had been under. She was adamant about not going back to their old church and, although it was hard for Ed to leave, they began meeting regularly for church with us in Lorette.

One Sunday after the message I called Ed to come forward.

I began to speak about Romans 12:1-3, renewing your mind. "I'm going to pray for you," I said, "that God would heal your mind and open His Word to you so that you can speak the mysteries of the gospel." I placed my hand on his shoulder and turned to our small congregation.

"Watch," I said to them, "see what God is going to do for this man."

I prayed a short simple prayer and let him go. The Word had gone out and it would not come back void.

The change in Ed was a miracle to behold. He began to grow by leaps and bounds. He couldn't get enough of God. We continued to spend time together, not just doing Bible studies, but doing everyday things, and I began to speak into his life.

# Ed

The months that followed after Adam's prayer for me I refer to as a game of baseball. He was the bat and I was the ball.

God would use Adam to show me things in my life—things that needed changing. I've never seen discernment before like I've seen it operate through Adam. He would tell me things that were going on in my life, in my family, and in my work that I didn't even know were happening until I listened to him and looked, and saw that it was the truth.

He was telling me I didn't have control of my kids. He was telling me my wife was doing things behind my back that I didn't know about. He was telling me I wasn't handling my finances right. Over and over he would come at me and hit me with something. I would be so angry! He'd push me right to the edge… but I just could not turn my back on the things he would show me. I was growing, and as I grew, God was shaping me—moulding me into the man He wanted me to be—but that growth was painful.

"Ed!" Adam said to me one day. "How is it possible that I went my whole life with a grade two education and never wrote an NSF check, but you've got grade seventeen and you can't balance your checkbook?"

I could feel the familiar rebellion rising up in me. Who was he to tell me how to balance my check book? What right did he have to say those things?

"It wasn't my fault," I started to explain. I ran my own business and when I made checks to the government sometimes it would take months for them to cash them, and they would be large amounts of money. I never knew when I could expect those checks to be cashed.

"It's not your fault you couldn't count? You don't know how to add two plus two?" Adam interrupted me. He pulled out his check book. "Whenever you write a check, subtract that sum from your balance."

"I don't have time to—"

"You need to know the exact amount of money you have, not just what the current bank balance shows. Account for *every* check. It's so simple." He threw his hands in the air. He was mad at me.

I felt my face go red. I turned and left his house, I needed to get away before I said or did something I would regret.

That night I sat beside my bed and thought through my response to Adam. He wanted to help me, and it was true I hadn't known the actual balance of my account because even though it showed the current money, it didn't show what part of that money was already spoken for. I should have had my checkbook balanced, but in this age—who even does that?

Instead I found an app. I vowed from then on I would never write another NSF check. Every time I spent, I logged it into the app and it did the balancing for me.

CHAPTER SIXTY-SIX

## REAPING THE REWARDS

**Adam**

Ed was growing, but it wasn't easy on him—it wasn't easy on me either! I didn't want to tell him the things the Lord was showing me, but at the same time, I knew it was for his benefit. We were spending a lot of time together, and more importantly, he was helping me build Shiloh.

Ed would put in a full day of work with his construction company and then he'd pack up his tools and drive out to St. Labre to meet me. I was spending nearly all my time there now, fixing up the yard, planting trees, hauling out the junk piles, burning down the outbuildings and cleaning up the scrap that seemed to be everywhere.

I'd be on the big mower when a thought would come to me.

"Ed!" I'd call him over and I'd tell him things about the scripture, about the kingdom of God, about daily life—whatever the Lord spoke to me I would tell him.     Together we worked at Shiloh and watched the cabin take shape.

### Ed

There was something about building Shiloh that had me wanting to go back there. I'd be putting in long hours all day at work, but when I'd get home I would have this urge to keep going. I'd pack up my tools and trailer and take off with my family to Shiloh. On weekends we'd bring a camper and spend all weekend there working.

I couldn't get over the blessings that were overflowing in my life as a result of this work. I didn't have my own house yet, but as I built Shiloh I began to make more money at my work than I ever had made before. I took off three full months to finish building the cabin and that year I made the most money I had ever made. It was as if God was paying me for my work—I had no need of anything.

Not only was I blessed financially, I began to receive healing in my life as well.

I had always had a bad back. This curse seemed to be in my family. Many people in my family have had multiple surgeries trying to fix their backs. I can remember having back pain since I was a kid. Anything I would try to do would always end up hurting my back. I lived with this pain as my constant companion. Over the years I just got used to it being there.

One day we were having a work day with the church, planting trees at Shiloh. My back was so sore I had to stop and take a break.

"Adam," I said, watching him planting the trees. "You have no idea how bad my back hurts right now."

Adam came over to me and sat down beside me.

"That's not a problem," he said.

I looked over at him. It was definitely a problem. It *hurt*.

"God can heal your back." He shrugged as he said it, like it would be nothing for God.

That evening after everybody had left, I stood by the kitchen window looking out, and began to think about what Adam had said about God being able to heal. I knew God was real now. He had been working in my life and, as I thought about his power to heal, there was an urge that rose up in me to cry out to God. A faith came over me, the faith of Jesus.

"Lord," I said, "you died on the cross for my salvation— and by your stripes we are healed! You've healed my finances, you've healed my mind, and I know you have paid for my back too! Why don't you heal me?" It was not a question of why he hasn't but more of a plead for it to happen now.

I locked up the cabin and got into my truck to drive home, praising God and worshipping him for what he had done. If the pain was still there I did not notice. The faith in me was greater than the pain. My inner man knew the work had been done. I drove and talked to God and by the time I got home, I realized it was gone. That's it. It just left—and it's never come back.

## CHAPTER SIXTY-SEVEN

# THE MOUNTAIN

The man who had first introduced me to church (now the Ekklesia fellowship) decided he was leaving. He and his family had been with us for several years and seeds of discontentment had started to grow.

"I'm leaving and I'm taking my family with me," he said to me at last.

"Look," I said, "I don't own you or anybody else here and I sure don't want to. I won't stop you from leaving."

Gabriel, one of the man's sons, stood and watched us talk. I could see the conflict in his face. He was only eighteen, but I could tell he listened hungrily to the messages I spoke.

It's hard to speak the truth to people I love. This man had been with me since the beginning and had stood up for me and stood beside me through much adversity. I knew though, that I had to be true to what God had given me to preach. Preaching the gospel was always likely to upset and offend some people. That's why I knew the church of God would be small.

The next Sunday I expected his whole family to be gone, but when I got there, Gabriel was sitting in the same place he always sat and his two sisters were with him.

I came up to him to shake his hand. "You're still here!" I said.

He smiled somewhat timidly. "I've never learned so much in my life as I have the past few months with you," he explained to me. "I knew either I had to accept you as a prophet sent from God, or denounce you and move on." He shrugged. "But you're the only one I've ever seen God work through. Your messages are not always easy, but they are true and they are always backed by the scripture, and the signs follow you!"

Wow! His small speech blew me away. This boy had gone against his parents to stay with me. I felt truly blessed.

After that day, Gabriel came to me once wanting to talk to me about some issues he was struggling with in his life.

"I keep asking God to change me," he said, "but no matter what I do, I'm the same. I can't fix this problem."

I leaned back in my chair and looked at him. I knew the problem was nothing for God to fix—in fact, it had already been done. But sometimes in life we have something required of us. Gabriel didn't believe the authority he had in Christ.

"I'll tell you what," I said. I leaned forward and I spoke right into his spirit. "Stop talking to God about your mountain and start talking to the mountain about your God."

His face looked stunned. He sat there for a moment and I could see the understanding and the *belief* dawn on his face.

"That's exactly right!" he said. I could see the excitement in him. "I know God is bigger than this mountain in my life, but I've been so focused on having *him* move it, I've forgotten that he's given me the authority to say, 'be moved.'"

It was that moment of belief that did it. He was set free from the mountain in his life because he believed the promises of God. Jesus said to his disciples: "For verily I say unto you, that whosoever shall say unto this mountain, Be thou removed, and be thou cast into the sea; and shall not doubt in his heart, but shall believe that those things which he saith shall come to pass; he shall have whatsoever he saith." (Mark 11:23)

So often we beg God for things that he's already done because we don't believe he's done them. Or we don't take authority over the enemy because we don't believe we can.

Ever since Gabriel believed that he had the divine authority to command his mountain to be moved, it immediately left. He did not even speak the words. He just believed it in his heart and it was done.

A few years later, I approached Gabriel about a problem he had been struggling with. He had a spirit that would prevent him from speaking the things God wanted him to say. After confronting him about the spirit, he agreed that he needed deliverance. At this point, I knew God would set him free from this.

The following Sunday morning, I prayed for Gabriel at church, rebuking the spirit that was making him mute.

He has been with me over ten years now and the change in him has been unbelievable. He now speaks freely in church and has even begun preaching.

CHAPTER SIXTY-EIGHT

## DEFYING GRAVITY

It was a hot summer day—a perfect day to go quading through the Sandilands. My friend Devin had come out to visit from Roblin, so I decided to take him to Shiloh to go for a quad ride.

Devin had brought out his big King Quad. It weighed about 700 lbs and had ample space for two people. I hopped on the back and directed him where to drive.

Quading near Shiloh is something to behold. The bush is full of pines and spruce with bluffs of cedars, oaks, poplars and birch trees. There's a marshy area with beaver dams, cattails, and willow reeds. There are sand dunes that surface between the pines and there are outbreaks of berries nearly everywhere. As a child we would be sent out into this bush to trap, hunt prairie chickens, or pick berries—and we were always accompanied by fear. Fear of predators. Fear of getting lost or hurt. But on a quad that all seemed so distant. This wasn't a chore—it was pure bliss. How things had changed since those early days.

"Careful!" I cautioned Devin as we neared a creek that meandered through the brush, "there's a bridge just over that way." I pointed to the left where a rickety old bridge hung across the water—a sharp incline up the creek bank waited at the end of the bridge.

Devin opened the throttle and we sped to the bridge. I felt the quad bump and jerk across the uneven planks of wood and then everything seemed to be in slow motion. He gunned the engine up the incline and as we went up I thought, '*he should have let me off first, we're going to tip this thing*'. It was too late—the quad was up in the air. I felt Devin's body falling back into mine and the quad falling on top of us. I reached my hands around him and gripped the quad, pushing it into the air. It was like gravity left us for that moment. The quad flew up from my push as if it weighed nothing, and Devin and I dropped sideways, landing on the bridge. The quad dropped about ten feet over on its side and I quickly got there and tipped it upright.

No one was hurt too badly, the quad was fine. We sat there thinking '*how the heck did that happen?*' I knew what should have happened. We should have flipped and been pinned under the quad, but instead we were standing on the bridge and staring at the 700 pound machine that I had somehow thrown off of us. I think of Samson and the pillars he took down. That was a strength that came from God. It's not natural. It's supernatural. Gravity had no pull on me in that moment I pushed the quad into the air, I knew it was a miracle—physically I could not have done that.

I stood back and marvelled at the protection of God and how He looks after His children. How many examples in my life did I have of God protecting me?

I remember a job I had taken back when I still had Adam's Underground. I had gone alone to repair an underground pipe. I dug a ten foot hole with a backhoe and climbed down into it with an old ladder. I knew it wasn't safe—I hadn't shored the walls of the hole. This was just a quick little repair job. I remember getting to the bottom of the hole and finding the pipe. My whole body was tense and alert as I kept glancing at the walls of mud around me. They might cave in at any second. It was stupid, doing this alone. Many people have died from having these holes collapse on them. My own cousin had died, buried in a collapsed hole. I quickly replaced the pipe piece I needed to and climbed the ladder back into the open air. I had no sooner pulled the ladder out of the hole and turned to head to my truck when I heard a *whoosh*. I looked behind and saw the hole completely caved in. There wasn't a two foot indent left in the ground. I would have been buried alive if God had not intervened.

Another memory of the Sandilands flashes into my mind. I was much younger. My brothers and I were racing our cars down one of the old gravel roads, going foolishly fast. I was driving one car with my brother and the other car held two other brothers. We were coming to a stretch where I knew I'd have a chance to pass my brothers' car, which was slightly in the lead. I gunned the gas and pulled out from behind him, too late to see that there was an oncoming vehicle headed right for us. Just as I was going into shock my brothers' car hit a puddle. The muddy water splashed over my windshield and I couldn't see anything. I hit the wipers to clear the mud and in those few seconds before the glass was clear again suddenly I was in front of their car and the oncoming vehicle whipped by completely untouched. My car was lifted up over my brothers' and set down again in the space of a few seconds. The Lord showed me what could have happened in that accident. I saw my car smashed like an accordion, and all of us lying dead in the wreckage. God had saved my brothers' lives and he had saved me.

CHAPTER SIXTY-NINE

# LEGACY

For the next ten years I laboured over the church and the people God had entrusted to my care. I opened the Word to them. I taught them, guided them, loved them, and provided for them in any way I could, and during that time God taught, guided, loved and provided for me.

I learned much during those years: patience, generosity, and how to be bold in the words Jesus gives me to speak. I want them to make it. I want them to endure. I want to see them in the Kingdom of God—what a reward that would be! And even as I know my time as their pastor is coming to an end (God is calling me onwards) I still strive to provide for them.

Shiloh will be a place of refuge and protection for their future.

God takes such good care of his children.

## Ed's Testimony of Healing

Just after I had started my construction company in 2003, I was diagnosed with Hypoglycemia. I would be working hard, usually in the mornings, and my body would start sweating. I would start shaking and lose all my energy. It started quickly and would increasingly get worse until I could ingest some form of sugar.

One day I was working at Shiloh with Adam when out of the blue he called me over. He casually put his hand on me and prayed, "Lord, take that thing from him and heal him."

That "thing" was the Hypoglycemia I had been living with. Adam didn't even know how to pronounce the word but God knows. That's what amazes me about Adam, he's different and yet God loves him because he loves God. And that's all that is required; that we believe in Him and love Him, nothing complicated and deep.

Weeks passed by and one morning I was at work grabbing some lumber to move. We had been working hard all morning and I was certain I would be getting an attack soon. Lunch break arrived and nothing had happened. This was the first time I stopped to think about it—*I haven't had a Hypoglycemic attack since Adam prayed for me!*

I worked harder, testing my body, and still, nothing happened.

I worked quite hard at simulating the triggers to create the perfect setting, but for weeks after, I could not. I had been healed!

Several years later, I was working on my knees on a deck. That afternoon my knees started to hurt and both of them became extremely sensitive and inflamed. They hurt on the inside and on the outside. I could not bend down on either knee because it was too painful. I could not climb stairs or a ladder without pain. They were in bad shape.

I went to see a doctor and I was prescribed some cream and advised to take some anti-inflammatory pills. I did all this, but after a few weeks the problem was still there. I was not worried about whether or not God would heal me. I had already been healed twice from some major problems and God would gladly take this from me as well. So, although I did not worry, the pain was there.

One day I was visiting Adam and I thought that he should know, we are friends and I can tell him anything. I told him that my knees hurt. Immediately he came and sat beside me and puts his hand on my knee and prayed for me.

Two or three weeks passed and nothing changed. I went to see Adam about something and he asked how things were with my knees. I told him that they still hurt and that was the end of that conversation.

Later that month, Adam and I were on our way to a meeting with the RM of Ritchot and he told me that God *did* heal me and that if I'm not healed its because I don't believe. I remember thinking to myself *'Of course I believe in healing, I've already experienced it.'* But he told me that sometimes God requires something of you. The first two times there was nothing required, but this time there was. He told me that I needed to believe with the inner man and not with the flesh. That I can't make it happen, the faith will be from God and I will have nothing to do with it.

This was a bit strange to me. God requires something of me and yet there's nothing I can do? How does that work?

The next day I was in the shower thinking about what was told to me and I started talking to my God. As I'm talking to Him and worshipping, the Spirit stirred in me and I heard Him say, *'you are healed!'*

I was healed, and I believed I was healed because my inner man had faith! It was given to me when I became completely dependant on Grace. I experienced something new and I grew in grace. My head and my flesh could do nothing for me, but God does it all. Not because I am good, but because He is good.

⚜

## The following are a few testimonials from people whose lives have been impacted by Adam's preaching:

I met Adam about twelve years ago when I heard him preach at a different church. I disagreed with all he said, but he backed everything up with scriptures I couldn't refute. My life personally, financially, and spiritually was a mess. Adam asked me to come over and asked me, "Do you believe in the Lord God? And I want the truth." (I was a liar and always dodged issues) I answered truthfully at last, "No, I don't." His reply was "Good! Between now and tomorrow salvation is going to come to you."

I didn't believe, but I knew that if twenty-four hours and one minute passed and nothing happened to me I would know this man was a fake.

The next morning at church, Adam was singing a song "Jesus sees you with his heart, not his eyes" when suddenly a huge presence of love came into the church. I doubled over on the ground crying and saying, "Thank you Jesus". Adam asked me to the front of the church and prayed for my ears to be opened and preached the sermon for me. I understood every word, I saw God speaking through the man and heard him say, "Philip, I love you."

I was at peace with the Lord God and felt no condemnation despite all my sins. They had all been forgiven.

Since then my personal life has changed totally. My finances have done a 180 degree turn. God has given back everything I had lost and more. More importantly, I have a heavenly Father who loves and care for me and I have a brother, Adam, who I love very much—A man who is used by God to care for me and love me and who is also used by God to correct me when I go wrong. I thank him very much for the good work God has used him for in my life.

Since being touched by God on September 6th, 2009, it's been the most exciting time of my life.— Philip

God is alive in Adam's life, and it impacts those around him. God working through Adam has changed me in ways I never could have imagined. Over the years, God has used Adam to change my way of thinking and to help me understand things in the Bible I always used to wonder about. Through Adam I began to see a God who is alive and real and can work in your life. A God who doesn't reject you because of problems in your life, but a God who accepts you the way you are and takes on the responsibility of cleaning you himself. A God who cares and sees when you are hurting. There were times when I felt so alone and wondered if God cared or heard me. God used Adam to show me that he does hear and care, at exactly those moments when I needed it the most. There is such a caring love and tenderness in Adam, and I know that's not his character, it's something God put in him that shines through. From the preaching I have heard through Adam, I have a hope to keep me going. I wouldn't have that hope if God hadn't worked in his life the way he had.—Abigail

Adam has been like a father to me, a mentor, a teacher, a leader, and a better friend than anyone could ever ask for. It's a scary thought when I look back at all the things I've been through in my life and wonder where I would be if Adam was never there to guide me through it all. I believe with all my heart that it was God that made our paths cross and I am forever thankful for it. I'm the type of person that has a hard time opening up to people, but I can honestly say that I love that man to pieces and appreciate all that he has ever done for me. I just don't say it enough. —Devin

After many years of wandering from church to church to church, I got to a place of knowing I had nothing, after over twenty years of believing I was 'saved'. I was scared and desperate and I cried to God and He answered my cry. He led me to Pastor Adam.

The first time I heard him preach, I knew my wandering was over. HE WAS DIFFERENT. The messages he receives from God by the Holy Spirit, he speaks with conviction, authority, and passion. God has changed my life, taken me out of the mess I was in (my old life) and shown me the hope that is in Christ (when I had none) through the guidance and caring of Pastor Adam.

God has healed me of long-standing physical problems and He has used me to help others, so I know my God is real! I thank Him for sending Pastor Adam to teach us.—Deb

Before I ever met Adam I was filled with confusion, questions, and with an incredible desire for truth. From the first time I heard him speak I knew there was something in him that I so craved. He spoke words into my life and I knew, for the first time in my life, this was the truth. Because of the truth, I have been able to experience God, I have been set free, I have been healed, and I have seen the spirit of God at work. I have been changed into a completely different person. —Cathrene

❧✠☙

Adam lives his life according to what he sees in scripture. As Jesus was an example to the disciples, so is Adam to me. There is nothing traditional or religious about the way Adam talks or works for the Lord. His connection with God will always put him 'on the money' with his encouragement and discipline, and it's never what you think or how you think it should be done. One of the biggest impacts that Adam has had in my life is the consistency with his own life. Year after year standing on the word of God, which never changes. Amidst our ever changing world, God will stay the same.— Jules

❧✠☙

Looking back over the twelve years I have known him, I can fully attest that Adam is a true messenger of God who speaks what he hears God speak. The words have always been for our benefit, always pointing towards the God that he serves and never toward himself. He is always humble, and never prideful. He has strongly exhorted the church to foster our very own relationship with God, leading us to become self-sufficient, having never to rely on a man or any other medium for spiritual nourishment. His greatest purpose for us was to see us flourish in Chirst, which was clearly demonstrated through his divine passion ,dedication, power and numerous personal convictions.—Gabriel

Pastor Adam is my Pastor, councillor, and friend. God has used him mightily in my life. He has spoken truth into my life that has set me free from bondage. When he prayed for me, I felt the Spirit of the Lord come into me and I could see a cage with a bird inside, and as he continued to pray the door of the cage was opened and the bird flew out! It was free! That was me—God had set me free and I felt and experienced a love, joy, and peace like I had never experienced in my whole life. God filled the emptiness in me. It wasn't until later on down the road that I realized I had also been healed from MS after that prayer! —Becky

When I first met Adam it was like that first gasp of air you have after being held under water for a long time. My eyes fastened on him and I couldn't look away. I watched him speak with such passion, authority, and *assurance* —as if he was speaking from the depths of his soul about something deeply real to him.

I had been struggling with all sorts of doubts and questions about faith and God and I was sick to death of the answers people had. No one was sure of anything and no one cared to do anything about it. I was overwhelmed with bitterness and anger from past experiences in my life, and I desperately wanted something real or I was ready to give up completely.

Seeing Adam speak with such passion and confidence opened my eyes to see he believed in a God, and he *knew* that God personally. Here in front of me at last was proof that God was real, and that He really did speak to people, and even if there were few, there were *some* people at least that had a connection to this God.

I kept grappling with my own doubts though, until at last in one of Adam's messages 'Just Believe' his words sunk through to me, and God set me free. He said 'either He did what He said He did (forgave our sins and gave us His righteousness) or He's a liar! Decide for yourself, did He do it? Or did He lie?' I was struck with the simplicity of it. Many of us don't believe the simple gospel, and the evidence is in our actions. I 'believed' my whole life that Christ paid for my sins, yet for some reason I carried them around like heavy burdens, unwilling to let them go. When I heard that line, 'Did He do it or is he a liar?' I couldn't say He was a liar—I knew He had done it—and I just believed! Those burdens fell away like they were nothing! I was a totally changed person.

God has continued to use Adam in my life. The Bible talks about 'He that receiveth a prophet in the name of a prophet shall receive a prophet's reward" and I have seen that first hand in my life. Spending time with Adam and accepting that God has placed him in my life to help me has showered my life with blessings. Just being able to write this book and have a small glimpse into the relationship Adam has with God has changed me.

I long to be able to experience all that God has for me, and I'm so excited that I see my God working in my life, and through my life. I hope that others who read this book will be able to see that God is real, and can have real relationship with His children.

Adam is proof that the people of God will not be perfect in the flesh, but they will be the people that have the Spirit of God working through them, doing supernatural things, and bringing the kingdom of God to men here on Earth. I want to be one of those people, as Adam is. —Valeda Verrier

# EPILOGUE

It's dark outside but warm. I'm sitting under a thousand stars, gazing up at the firmament and thinking about my past. Remembering is not easy. It takes courage and strength, but I have never been one to take the easy route. I lean back in my chair and feel overwhelmed by the work God has done in my life. It's not often that I let my mind drift back to my past, to all the pain it carries, but tonight I feel the memories so close to me, like they're hanging over me just waiting to be revisited.

You wouldn't have recognized this place sixty years ago—and you certainly wouldn't have recognized me—a scrawny little kid with patched, worn clothes and no shoes.

This place where I sit now is a haven of peace and rest, but it wasn't always this way. Even now I can picture clearly how the farm used to look. How run down it was, full of holes and ruts, old discarded equipment lying in heaps, hidden by weeds and tall overgrown grasses. The shoddy house that was grey with weathered boards, the patched roof and sagging steps, the barn where the cows and horses slept, and the patchwork fences we were forever mending.

I can see my mom kneeling on the floor at night, clutching her rosary, crying while saying her prayers, and my dad sitting by the radio listening to the French CKSB radio smoking a cigarette. My brothers and I would lie curled up in the attic, a tangle of arms and legs. A donated pile of old jackets was our only cover. We'd huddle together until morning.

The old woodpile is the only thing that still stands from those days. I kept it because it was a symbol of safety to me as a child. When I was scared or sad or hurting, I'd go to the woodpile and hide there and talk to God. I didn't know it then, but He was watching me. He heard my cries, He saw my pain, and He knew my fear. I have had much of all three of those things in my life, but I wouldn't trade any of it for what I have now.

*Are you real God?*

That had been the desperate cry of my heart when I was just nineteen. My life had been so empty. I had felt so alone in the world.

I remember getting into fights just wishing someone would hit me so that I could cry and let out some of the loneliness that was pent up inside me. But when God first spoke to me that day in the mud, it had been the beginning of a long and beautiful journey.

My life now couldn't be fuller. God says in his Word to prove Him, and see if He will not open the windows of heaven and pour out a blessing you cannot contain. This is not talking about money, although he's certainly blessed me in all areas. It's talking spiritually.

I'm so full—my life is full of the blessings of God. Everywhere I look I see His hand, His work in my life. The wisdom He has given me: the messages. If I preached every day from now until I die I wouldn't be able to preach all the messages God has given me.

Me, a boy who didn't get past grade two, who didn't speak English, who was told his whole life he was good for nothing. God saw that child and the hunger I had for truth and wisdom and understanding. He reached down and touched me, He healed my mind, opened my understanding, and opened His Word to me.

I've been so blessed.

When my parents first sold the farm they sold it to one of my older brothers. I remember my mom saying, "Whatever you do, don't let Art get ahold of the homestead. He'll make a church out of it!" Well, when they passed away I bought the farm from my family.

Shiloh. That's what I named the farm, a place of peace.

# GOD, ARE YOU REAL?

Now the farm is beautiful: the old house and barn burned, the old sheds and outbuildings destroyed, the yard cleaned and levelled, and now the driveway long, straight and lined with trees. The yard is tidy and landscaped with an orchard, a garden, and a gazebo.

Even now as I close my eyes I can hear the soft rustle of the leaves in the breeze and the gentle rattle of their branches. During the day the yard is a sanctuary for birds, flitting from tree to tree or perching on the feeders.

Most striking of all is the cabin—set just where the old house used to be—it's a retreat now. A large front porch welcomes all who come. The walls are lined with windows and the inside is open and inviting, with nooks for coffee, music or games. Many services have been held here, many conversations, and most importantly: the fellowship of friends and family.

It is no longer a place of hurt—but of healing.

"Hi, my sweet," The screen door opens and slams shut as Edie comes outside to sit with me. My wife, a true gift from God, has stuck beside me through many hard times.

"You know," I said to her as she pulled up a chair next to mine, "God has been so good to me."

"*Yes*," she waited for me to continue.

"I wish everyone would know him. I wish everyone would come to that point where they ask *God are you real?* And mean it from the depth of their souls. He is real. Just look at my life. At the miracles." Edie had experienced first hand some of the miracles I was referring to. "It's so good," I said, "to walk with God."

I looked back into the night sky and felt the breeze on my skin. "I've looked back on my life," I said, "but now it's time to look forward." I could feel an excitement in me. "If we only knew the things God has in store for us. How He plans to use us in the age to come."

"Yes," Edie said, squeezing my hand in hers.

I felt like Moses, when he walked up the mountain at the end of his days to be with God. He had given all he had, done all he could to be a faithful servant of God, leading the Israelites through the desert towards the promised land could not have been an easy task. *Be strong and of good courage* he had said to Joshua, as he was leaving.

God had prepared me many years in order to shepherd this church and even though they were small in number, I knew God had called and drawn each one of them. I considered myself blessed to be used by God as a messenger of his Word to these people. I had spent many years working with the church God had given me, but now I knew the time was fast approaching when I would be leaving. I entrusted that small little group of people into God's hands and I hoped I had been faithful.

"Ever increasing faith," I said, "that's what God requires from us. The more experiences we have with him, the more our faith grows."

My faith now felt limitless. My work was far from done. There were still more people to meet, more hearts searching for God, lost in darkness and deception, and my own heart burned for them. My desire was to help people, to turn the hearts of the children towards their Father, and turn the heart of the Father towards His children.

This physical life is short, but there is a life after this one for our inner man, and that is eternal. Looking ahead now, I fully expect more great and exciting things from my Father and my friend.

## ABOUT THE AUTHOR

Adam lives in Steinbach, Manitoba. He spends his time singing country songs, picking tunes on his guitar, and has even recorded several music CDs with his friends. He collects antique cars and if there is a car show around, he will most likely be there. Adam is a pastor/evangelist at heart and his greatest joy comes from talking to people about the Lord. There is a famine in the land today, not of water or of bread, but of hearing the Word of God. He and his wife, Edie, are always looking for people to talk to and opportunities to share with others the goodness and truth of God. When they aren't at Shiloh, they spend much of their time between Canada and the United States forging relationships and witnessing to those who are searching.

They plan on visiting churches across North America in the future to share their story and their hope in the one true God.

To invite Adam to your church or organization
Email edieadam@mymts.net for more information or
Call Adam 204-392-6767

Made in the USA
Monee, IL
15 December 2021